C000133102

Grant Smith tells it how it is.
engaging, moving and amu
transform the lives of poor pe
of refusing to be downcast by disappointment or overco
Social enterprise is about making money by doing good: Grant Smith
shows how.

RICHARD HIGGINSON
CHAIR, FAITH IN BUSINESS

This incisive exploration of injustice and one man's call to use his skills to
help those who need them most is a reminder that each of us has a part to
play in turning God's world the right way up. As someone who has seen
first-hand the problems that poverty in Africa causes, I welcome Grant
Smith's commitment to doing something about it. This is a rallying call to
all of us to strive for dignity, equality and justice for all; and a challenge
not just to teach a person how to fish, but to equip them to buy the pond.

AMANDA KHOZI MUKWASHI
CEO, CHRISTIAN AID

Have you ever asked yourself what an ordinary working professional or
small business owner like yourself can do to make a difference in the face
of injustice and poverty? Read Grant's story about doing something –
not everything, admittedly, but something quite amazing – and discover
the power that business can have to transform the lives of families,
communities and nations. With his down-to-earth humour and gripping
honesty, Grant tells a story of trial and error, success and failure, through
thick and thin. His journey to becoming an accidental entrepreneur will
draw you in and inspire you for your own adventure. In Grant's own
words, 'God hadn't asked me to become a marine biologist, he asked
me to do what I am good at and use it for a bigger end game.' How do
you become an accidental social entrepreneur? You say *yes* to God, *no* to
injustice and *yes* to putting your business and professional skills to work
for God's kingdom work.

JO PLUMMER
CO-FOUNDER, BUSINESS AS MISSION RESOURCE TEAM AND CO-CHAIR,
BUSINESS AS MISSION GLOBAL

The Accidental Social Entrepreneur will no doubt be a favourite pick for anyone keen to know the raw, unedited and behind-the-scenes story of entrepreneurs. Grant Smith lets us in on his journey as he seeks to do his part in being a solution to our world, a mandate that behoves each of us. As you read through the book, you meet the real Grant! Fortunately, he does not project himself as Mr Superman. You will read about a man who is genuinely seeking to live his life to the full; a man who diligently seeks to execute his kingdom mandate; a man who works hard to be a solution for the needy and yet not a burden to his friends and networks. A lot of people seek the easy and hassle-free route in helping those in need in society, but not Grant Smith. He does not carry a begging bowl around. In fact, I know him more as a businessman than as part of an NGO personnel. His business acumen is the muscle he uses to propel his charity initiatives at Hand in Hand. You will certainly enjoy Grant's personality and pathos in narrating his stories about working in the African region.

I highly recommend this book, not just to entrepreneurs but to anyone who has been entrusted with leadership. It is real, infused with witty personality and yet carries serious practical business truths. It's loaded with lessons of what has worked and what has not. It lays Grant's journey in entrepreneurship bare, letting us in on all the nitty-gritty aspects of business.

DANIEL KAMAU
CEO, FUSION CAPITAL

This book has to be the most honest and raw account I have ever read of an adventure with God. Grant's account of his experiences mixed with the reality of his thoughts and feelings as he walks through the ups and downs of being a social entrepreneur is a challenge for those of us who wish to venture into this space. His vulnerability and celebration of failure as learning is an encouragement and learning tool for us all.

JOANNE O'CONNOR
DIRECTOR, JUNCTION 42

If you hate reading manuals, then you will love *The Accidental Social Entrepreneur*. Grant Smith describes his unplanned journey into kingdom entrepreneurship in a refreshing 'I don't want to put the book down' style. He is blatantly honest about both his successes and failures. Along his journey, he touches on fundamental truths we should never ignore. He gets to the root causes of poverty to find sustainable solutions and is never satisfied with a box of Band-Aids. From the basics to dealing with corruption, fundraising from unusual institutional investors, working out very big wrinkles and knowing when to stop, his stories are great. The lessons he has learnt along the way are relevant and presented in everyday language.

You will not know you are reading a manual on kingdom-building but you will learn to want to trust God for his faithfulness. Grant's mantra is to never conclude that God cannot be trusted, and it is a recurring theme in all of his stories. You will retell his stories to your friends – they are worth retelling.

WILLY KOTIUGA
PHD, PROGRAMME DIRECTOR, LAUSANNE GLOBAL WORKPLACE FORUM;
CHAIR, BAKKE GRADUATE UNIVERSITY BOARD OF REGENTS;
FORMER SENIOR DIRECTOR, SNC-LAVALIN

The Accidental Social Entrepreneur is a sober account of the stark realities of the challenge of doing business in Kenya. Grant shares candid stories of both perseverance and failure that the Hand in Hand Group have experienced as they seek to do business justly. Financial failure or success are not the only determinants of a good business.

REVD DR DENNIS TONGOI
FOUNDER AND DIRECTOR (RTD) OF CMS-AFRICA

What a read! I can hear Grant through and through, passionate about making the difference to more than 3,000 Kenyans. This is one person's story of challenge and hope as Grant makes life count as a Christian. Integrity runs through the pages as he strives to make a sustainable difference to the lives of young people in Kenya. Making life count as an imperfect Christian. Seriously Epic.

TIM ROSE
NON-EXECUTIVE DIRECTOR, BAPTIST INSURANCE COMPANY, BIBLE
SOCIETY RESOURCES LTD., VEREIN BAPTIST THEOLOGICAL; CHAIR,
DIOCESE OF CHELMSFORD VINE SCHOOLS TRUST; CHARTERED DIRECTOR,
INSTITUTE OF DIRECTORS AND MANAGING DIRECTOR OF GROWBRIDGE LTD

I have several reasons for why I would commend this book to those seeking to be faithful to God in their Christian living, but I choose to give only three of them. First, the book is highly readable, giving several short life stories that are interesting to follow. Secondly, the book is one flowing, challenging story of the life and faith of Grant Smith relating with several people as he seeks to obey God in serving the needy. Thirdly, I have lived through several of the stories written here, and I very much appreciate the high level of honesty, transparency and vulnerability depicted by Grant. You will be challenged to think and live your faith meaningfully in every circumstance you meet in life.

PROF. TIMOTHY WACHIRA

Grant writes like he lives – with a 'no-holds barred' devotion to serving Jesus with his whole life. This book is so important because each page is honest and real and tells the story of what happens when a person wholeheartedly surrenders their life to Jesus. Grant challenges the 'familiar' and inspires us all to a deep devotion to Jesus in our daily lives. I dare you to read it!

REVD DENNIS PETHERS
FOUNDER AND INTERNATIONAL PIONEER, THE ROOFTOP MINISTRIES

A must-read for anyone who feels called to combine a life of giving with business. Grant Smith's adventures in South America and East Africa will both enlighten and entertain you. The good humour, generosity of spirit and simple faith he has shine through in his writing. He doesn't shy away from the difficulties he has faced, nor take himself too seriously. His impish sense of humour is always with you. I wish more business books were like his.

DR PHIL GOODWIN
EXECUTIVE CHAIRMAN, FUSION CAPITAL

Grant Smith is a passionate man who, in line with his faith, combines risk taking with natural gifting and skills to change lives. His desire to do the will of God is evident, as are the fruits of his kingdom-building life.

PAUL SZKILER
CEO, TRUESTONE IMPACT INVESTMENT MANAGEMENT

You'll hear Grant Smith's voice in these pages. It's authentic, honest and it'll make you smile. More than that, you'll hear his heart. It's the heart of someone who is not only bothered by injustice but is determined to do something about it – through business done well, in a way that makes a social difference but still makes money. In an account that's part business memoir, part theological reflection and part spiritual journey, Grant takes us through the lows and occasional highs of his adventures, all from the perspective that 'Christianity is a way of life, not an insurance policy for what comes next'. If that resonates with you, read on.

ANTONY BILLINGTON
THEOLOGY ADVISOR, LONDON INSTITUTE FOR CONTEMPORARY CHRISTIANITY; SENIOR PASTOR, BEACON CHURCH, ASHTON-IN-MAKERFIELD

Grant Smith delivers a fun approach to his experiences navigating from the commercial world to traditional charitable missions, and then returning to the commercial world for solutions which traditional charities are unable to provide. Excellent storytelling as multiple failures lead to an outstanding and God-pleasing outcome!

BILL MEIER
PRESIDENT AND CEO, KINGDOM WORKERS

Grant Smith has done an excellent job of bringing forth very confronting issues that are ignored by the media and painting a picture of the problems and poverty people are facing in Africa. Grant shares throughout the book very practical tips about building business for the kingdom and how one idea to create jobs has an amplified positive effect for so many people. I have personally been inspired to think out of the box about how we can help those in need through business.

SARAH-JANE MEESON
FOUNDER, CHRISTIAN WOMEN IN BUSINESS

The Accidental Social Entrepreneur by Grant Smith is a must-read for all Christian business people whether they work in the for-profit or non-profit sector. Grant's journey into social entrepreneurship is genuine and inspiring, and it provides a great example of what it means to be a faithful servant of God. The book is filled with stories that will resonate with many of us. It is full of the wisdom Grant has gained and the lessons he has learned through his experiences of both success and failure.

GENE KIM
EXECUTIVE DIRECTOR, CENTER FOR INTEGRITY IN BUSINESS, SEATTLE
PACIFIC UNIVERSITY

Wow this book is gold! Grant carries the heart of God directly to you. It is challenging, heart-wrenching and thought-provoking. Grant does not just share the principles of wealth creation and the challenges that go with them but the kingdom purposes of God. Grant is a solutionist who radically challenges the 'why' of making money. What is your why?

JANET GRACE SCHIER
AUTHOR OF TO HELL WITH DEBT! LET'S MAKE MONEY

Proverbs 29:18 says 'Where there is no vision, the people perish' (KJV)– Grant Smith has a Godly vision, and I trust that those who benefit from it will not perish.

C. RALPH HILTON
RICS CHARTERED BUILDING SURVEYOR

Grant Smith is an intrepid entrepreneur. Not only does he see opportunities where others see problems; he also has the fortitude to see his visions become reality. This book is a testament to the transforming power of whole-life discipleship within testing circumstances.

DR PETER S. HESLAM
TRANSFORMING BUSINESS, UNIVERSITY OF CAMBRIDGE

THE
ACCIDENTAL
SOCIAL
ENTREPRENEUR

THE
ACCIDENTAL
SOCIAL
ENTREPRENEUR

GRANT SMITH

Muddy
Pearl

Published in 2019 by
Muddy Pearl, Edinburgh, Scotland.
www.muddypearl.com
books@muddypearl.com

British Library Cataloguing in Publication Data
A catalogue record for this book is available from the British Library
ISBN 978-1-910012-50-5
Cover design and typeset in Minion by Revo Creative Ltd, Lancaster
Printed in Great Britain by Bell & Bain Ltd, Glasgow

CONTENTS

FOREWORD

This is a funny book.

Laugh out loud funny in pretty much every chapter.

It is also an inspiring book.

But you don't need to be an entrepreneur, or a businessperson, or a manager, or a leader, or a charity worker or even a Christian, for that matter, to be inspired by it. You just need to be a human being who would like to make the most of what you've been given for the sake of others.

This is not the story of how one extraordinary man struggled against insuperable odds to achieve extraordinary things for thousands of people. Quite the contrary. You don't get to the end of this book and think,

Yup, well, if I was as smart as Grant, as wise as Grant, if I had had Grant's education, Grant's capital, Grant's contacts, well then ...

No, it's an inspiring book because it's the story of how one person took the gifts and skills and relationships God gave him and set out to create as much opportunity for as many people in poverty as he and his wife Sue, and the people they gathered round them, possibly could.

And it's inspiring and funny because it's so refreshingly honest.

Grant is honest about how hard the road has been, how bewildering some of the failures, how mysterious some of the successes, or at least how mysteriously those successes came about. He's honest about the principles he's applied and how they didn't necessarily work. He's honest about his relationship with God, and what he's learned, and what is still a mystery.

The reason this book is funny, inspiring and honest is because that's what Grant is – in a down-to-earth, straight-talking, Scottish kind of way. I've known him for over 20 years. I 'taught' him at Bible college, though whether he learned anything useful from me is yet to be established. When he left, he asked me if I would meet with him for coffee once every 6 months and ask him awkward questions. He would pay for the coffee, I would try to be awkward and he would answer the questions. So I've been tracking Grant and Sue's story for a while now: one moment he's about to build a road from Zanzibar to Cairo and the next he isn't; one moment a development is about to be built and 3 years later it's still about to be built. One time he hasn't been paid for months and has almost no money at all in his personal account. And it's the same the next time too. On that occasion he may have let me pay for the coffee.

Last year I happened to be in Kenya for a conference and I got to meet the team who work for the Hand in Hand charity. I spent a day at the orphanage they support and a day meeting some of the farmer-grandmothers who cultivate micro-plots to keep their orphaned grandchildren alive – with the charity's help. Another day, I stood on the roof of the then not-quite-finished 10-storey CMS Africa building they'd helped to create, talking to one of the apprentices Grant's team had sponsored and pondering the massive difference the project would make to thousands of people.

Then I stood in a field on the edge of a city slum where a small team feed and teach a group of street children – they've been doing it for years. Afterwards, we went to a modest restaurant where the team who owned the land signed a development agreement with Grant and his Kenyan business partner that would mean housing would be built and that every one of those children, plus many, many more, would get a much better chance to realize their potential.

One thing has, in the end, led to another. And another. But not in a linear way. 1 step forward, 2 steps sideways; 1 step forward, no steps anywhere; 1 step forward, 4 leaps forward ... Indeed, what emerges from this gripping tale is the power of perseverance, the power of a godly passion for the benefit of others, the power of prayerfulness, the power and desire of a great God to work in his ways through his people for the benefit of others.

So, when you get to the end of this book, yes, you will probably think Grant has used his life well – but you are also very likely to ask yourself what God wants you to do with what he's given you. And you are very likely to believe that he might make more of it than you could ever have imagined before.

Mark Greene
LICC
March 2019

THE BIT BEFORE THE BOOK BEGINS

There are many people who I need to say thanks to, but of course as soon as I do that, I will upset those I didn't say it to. You will soon read about the people who have influenced me and helped to get Hand in Hand Group (HiHG) to where it is now, so I won't bother with most of them here. I have actually changed lots of people's names in this book. That is not because I have forgotten them; it's because most people have requested that they remain anonymous. Then I forgot who said what, so decided to change nearly all of them. Then there are the people that have actually helped to transfer my ideas from my laptop into a readable story. Dave has played a large part on that front; Dave is a good friend, a journalist and gave me some valuable advice early on.

Then there is Emma. Emma initially worked for HiH charity and then, as the business grew, moved over to working with me at HiHG. I once read a book called *The Leader Who Had No Title*,[1] and Emma really was an employee with no title. Officially, she was my PA, but that

1 Robin Sharma, *The Leader Who Had No Title: A Modern Fable on Real Success in Business and in Real Life* (Simon & Schuster: 2010).

doesn't describe either what she did or her input into the business. Emma has read most of this book because she didn't want me upsetting people like I did in my last one. So if you are upset by this one, email Emma – it's her fault, not mine. But Emma, thank you. Since I started writing this book, and as the months have passed, Emma has actually left HiHG and has started walking her own path, but I am so grateful for all of her help.

Then there is Charity. (It's confusing enough trying to keep your charity separate from your business, without having a lady called Charity working *in* your business!) Suffice to say, Charity has also helped me with this book, and her input has been invaluable. Thank you, Charity.

Then Stephanie of Muddy Pearl who has, in a way, coached me throughout the writing of this book, encouraging me to make the story stronger. As I got to know Stephanie – bit by bit – I realized that we had more in common than the desire to simply publish a book. Stephanie has her own story – obviously, we all do – but hers is a story which, in many ways, is the same as mine. This gave us a mutual understanding of what it is we were trying to tell. Thank you, Stephanie.

Mark – what do I say of him? Mark is the one who encouraged me to write this book and who introduced me to Stephanie. I am sure that without Mark's backing, my script would have never made it to the 'maybe' pile at Muddy Pearl. If you are ever suffering from low self-esteem, just get Mark to introduce you to someone and he will pour out all of your good attributes – some of which you weren't aware you even had. Thanks Mark.

And of course Sue: Sue is my best friend and my wife. I sometimes look at couples and think that one partner is in danger of holding the other back. For us, it's like Sue put me in a rocket launcher and lit the fuse. To say that Sue has changed my life is an understatement. She loves me, she is honest with me, she inspires me, she challenges me and she holds my hand. Without Sue, there would be no Hand in Hand Group and there would be no business. Somebody once said to me,

Sue is quite a risk taker.

I immediately thought it was a pop at her choice to marry me. But he went onto say,

If Sue wasn't a risk taker, she couldn't sleep in the same bed as a risk taker like you every night.

It's a fair point and an important one.

But Sue has an uncomplicated faith, some of which has rubbed off on me. So, thank you, Sue – I love you very much.

And the point of this book? If one of the consequences of reading it is that you become inspired to do something which can make a difference in just one person's life, then it will have been worthwhile. Believe me you can!

HELLO

I am a husband, father, brother, quantity surveyor, trustee, director, cyclist, cook – but I am not a writer. A dangerous place to start in the first paragraph of a book I want you to read. But I have a story.[2] And now, as I sit at the keyboard, I think I know what it is I am going to tell you ...

This story is about my journey over the last 20 years, during which I have launched 1 charity and several businesses, across 3 continents. To understand my story, you need to know that I am a Christian – and that means everything. But don't misunderstand that statement; I am no 'saint' – I am imperfect and I mess up like everyone else. But to me, Christianity is a way of life, not an insurance policy for what comes next.

My story has taught me that God can be trusted, but he doesn't half make it hard at times. Trusting God is not some fluffy, soft option: at times you really have to grit your teeth and hold on tight. Whatever your religious beliefs may be, at the end of this book I hope that you will see that ordinary people like you and me have been created for a purpose and have the potential to facilitate miracles. Finding that purpose will be the most fulfilling and exhausting experience of your life. And the most fun.

2 And, I am told, a quirky sense of humour!

~~~~~~

One day, I was on a date with a young lady. We had been for a walk in the park and were making our way back to my Capri 1600L with its black vinyl roof. As we approached the car, this young lady asked me,

Would you ever give up your career and go into Christian ministry?

Now 33 years ago, when I was asked that question, my understanding of Christian ministry was quite different to what it is today. Today, I understand that if we are disciples of Christ, then we are all in Christian ministry. But back then, to me, it meant giving up a well-paid job and becoming poor. I knew I didn't want that and wouldn't choose it. But, you see, I had a problem: my problem was that I knew that if I was truly a spirit-filled Christian, then the answer to that question had to be *Yes*. But I also knew that my real answer was *No*. The problem I now faced was that, up until this point in my life, nobody had asked me the question, and so I hadn't had to answer it. But now the question was asked and it demanded an answer.

And my answer was,

The real answer to your question is, No. *But I know that's not the right answer, so I am going to have to go away and think about it.*

What happened next was that I married the young lady, with the question unanswered. But I continued to battle with the question. I can remember digging my mother's garden in the springtime; I can remember ramming the fork into the soil, I can remember turning over a clod of mud, and each time I rammed the fork into the soil, asking the question,

Would I give up my career?
And each time as I turned the clod, the answer was,
No.
So I kept digging, hoping that eventually the answer would be, *Yes*, but it kept coming back, *No*. I wrestled with the question for 3 years until eventually, one day, in my heart of hearts, the truthful answer was *Yes*. My mum had the best-dug garden in Essex!!

So what had happened?

Because nothing actually changed at that point. I didn't give up my career, I didn't leave my job and I didn't go into 'ministry'. But fundamentally, something had shifted in my head and I knew that if needed, I *could* give up my career.

And my mum had the best-dug garden in Essex.

In 33 years a lot has happened. I have not changed my career. Yet. But I have, in a way, gone into 'ministry'. And yes, full time.

∿∿∿∿∿∿∿∿∿∿∿∿∿∿∿∿∿∿∿

I had imagined that I might put pen to paper, or fingers to keyboard, when Hand in Hand had become a success. Then Mark, who was one of my lecturers from Bible College and fellow squash player (who always, but always, beat me) told the story about his boss from the large American advertising agency he had once worked at who always said *hello* to the receptionist on his way in to work. This left such an impression that one day this boss was introduced to a secretary who responded,

Oh you're David Warden, you're the one who says, Good Morning *to receptionists.*

That simple, regular action obviously stood out because others did not say *Good Morning* to the receptionist. This has always stuck with me, and although I don't work for a large American advertising agency, I always say *hello* to the receptionist, the car park attendant, the cleaners, absolutely everyone – because I know that if Jesus were here, he would definitely say *hello* at the very least. Mark no longer works in a New York skyscraper with a receptionist, but he will still say *hello* to the cashier in a supermarket: by name, noticing their badge, and will ask them about their day. All of that to introduce Mark, who has now become my mentor.

Then, Mark said to me,

Hand in Hand will never be a success in your eyes, because there will always be more that can be done, so the book will never get written.

And he's obviously right. Because when I come to the conclusion that we are a success, it would suggest that the job is complete, and for the Christian, that can never be the case. At least not until the Lord returns. So where are we now?

Hand in Hand is a UK charity working in Africa. We support orphanages, a project for grandmothers and orphans, a vocational training centre and various other projects. The charity touches about 3,000 lives a year in various shapes and forms.

To help us do this, supporters in both the UK and Kenya give between £300k–400k year on year. Even during a double-dip recession (some say it's a triple dip, some say it's more than a dip; it's a nose dive heading for disaster). Dip or dive, this level of income has somehow been maintained and, in fact, shows signs of growing.

Is that success? I ask myself.

Not yet, I answer.

But that's 3,000 people who, in one way or another, are being supported to improve their lives through education or are assisted in their physical and spiritual needs, I argue.

But there are so many more, I remind myself.

More orphans, more grandmothers and more than 60% of the population of Nairobi living in slums.[3]

There is more need than our dedicated supporters can begin to support.

Our aim for these 3,000 people – at least – is to enable them to become independent. And more than that, it is to give them the foundation to provide for themselves and to have happy, fulfilling lives which in turn support others less fortunate than they eventually become.

This means that the grandchildren of the grandmothers we are currently supporting, and the orphans in the orphanage and the students at the schools and vocational centre, when they grow up and leave school and the vocational centre or even university, will need jobs. Jobs that are fairly paid, with reasonable conditions and hours, and a future.

And so there is the business – or businesses, to be precise – which are more difficult to explain. How is success measured? The number of products sold? The number of satisfied customers? The profit made? The number of people employed? These are all valid indicators, and if, say, we looked at the number of people employed – which

3 Kibera Facts & Information, https://www.kibera.org.uk/facts-info/ (Accessed 4 February 2019).

currently is somewhere in the region of 200 – you may not say we were much of a success. However, if we were to measure success by access to finance, this would be a different story, which I am coming to. Maybe the best way to explain it is the way I explained it to a potential investor a year or so ago.

Let's call him Jimmy.

I kind of got off on the wrong foot with Jimmy; a mix up over a phone call, if the truth be known, a note in the diary that I would ring on a certain day at a certain time, without being completely clear what I was going to say. At the start of our first ever conversation, Jimmy picks up on this and is ready to hang up on me there and then. But somehow we pull through and so I go to visit him in his rather ordinary offices above a shop on the high street.

After the usual pleasantries, Jimmy starts to question me. I give my answers cautiously, not really knowing his agenda. Jimmy asks me,

Why should I invest in your company? The houses you are building will end up getting built by someone, what makes you any different?

My response,

Because we take a child from a slum who has never known her father, whose mother died of preventable causes, who had no access to education or tools to equip her for the future, and we support that child through education and into university. Through our business we are now employing her as a quantity surveyor to build homes for the growing Kenyan middle class, which I am asking you to finance.

Jimmy's response,

> *That's interesting: when your back is against the wall your true heart emerges. Why didn't you tell me that when you walked through the door? You're a 'transformational development company'.*

My response,

> *Because we haven't got there yet.*

This is effectively where the Hand in Hand Group – a charity and businesses in relationship with each other – wants to end up. If you ask me what success looks like, it looks like a slum girl becoming the CEO of the largest building contractor in Kenya. It looks like an orphaned boy being given the opportunity to study agriculture and becoming a farm manager. It looks like a child, whose parents couldn't bring her up, being given the opportunity to learn a practical skill like plumbing and being properly paid for the value she adds to the houses we build. It looks like that same child then being able to afford her own home, bringing up her own children and enjoying a life in which she is not worrying every single hour of every single day about whether she and her family will eat tomorrow. It will look like Hand in Hand Group growing so large within Africa that our competitors will have to change their employment criteria if they are to keep their staff. The need for charity will be reduced because, instead of poorly-paid construction workers and farm workers coming to the charity for support for their children's school fees, they will pay those fees themselves because they are earning sufficient money to afford them. And no person working for Hand in Hand will be forced to live in a tin shed with no water, electricity, sewerage or dignity, fighting off the threat of pneumonia every time it rains because it gets so cold and damp that their lungs can't cope.

Yes, that is a 'transformational development company' but we are not there yet. As God gives us enthusiasm, strength, perseverance, finance and sheer doggedness, that is where we will end up.

DISASTERS AND ENTHUSIASM

Churchill is believed to have said that,

Success is the ability to move from one failure to another without loss of enthusiasm.

Let me tell you now that we have had our failures, and we have had our disasters. There was the company we set up to sell second-hand agricultural and earth-moving machinery to East Africa. Tendered for millions of pounds of work, we sold 1 JCB at cost and 2 excavators that we never got paid for (although we do have 7 acres of land somewhere in the Rift Valley if we can ever find them). There were the Joint Venture companies we set up to build roads across Africa; our UK partner pulled out on the day of tender submissions. Yes, we have had our disasters and as sure as night follows day, there will be more to come. But we still have our enthusiasm!

I was invited to lunch by one of our investors at a fancy hotel in Nairobi. Let's call this investor Paul. Paul comes across as a very laid-back character, but don't be fooled by this outward appearance. Paul is taking in everything you say, analyzing and processing it. Paul has worked with the big financial institutions in the UK and has since set up his own private equity fund. He is supposedly retired, but is clearly too young for that – not ready for the pipe and slippers by the fireplace, walking the dog or doing the crossword.

Paul had actually delayed his onward journey by a day – not just any day, but a Saturday – to have lunch with me. I know I can be entertaining, but somehow I knew that entertainment was not the purpose of our meeting. We commenced by talking about the weather, and the menu and other general small talk that neither of us were really interested in, but which is always said out of politeness or something, I'm not sure what.

So I said,

Pleasant as the conversation is, I know you didn't ask me here today to discuss the weather or the menu, or, come to that, to buy me a nice lunch. What did you want to tell me?

Paul basically had 2 points to make:

1. He completely believed in Hand in Hand's ability to make the current projects they were financing a success. This was more a reassuring statement than a newsflash.
2. They were prepared to back Hand in Hand financially for it to become the biggest contractor in Kenya, if that is where we wanted to go.

And the problem with that?

When I lie in bed at night and think about the fact that

Hand in Hand are not the biggest contractor in Kenya, I certainly can't use the excuse that we didn't have access to finance.

CHAPTER 1

PINHEADS AND POVERTY

or

WHY I STARTED A CHARITY

20 years ago I started a charity. There were many reasons at the time. I can't remember them all now, but here is one: injustice bothers me.

I have come to the conclusion that the world is full of some complete pinheads. Children at school who are spiteful bullies, carjackers, people who will pick your pocket at any opportunity, people who drive big expensive cars and, because they drive big expensive cars, think they can push little cars out of the way, people who throw a small tip at a poor person, pastors who steal the tithes of the poor, drug dealers who lead young children into addiction, pimps who profit from good-looking girls, factory owners who pay their workers 50p a day so that they can make themselves millions, fly tippers, people who come home from holiday and laugh about how cheap everything was, gossips, politicians, people who wear designer sunglasses and don't take them off indoors, people who shout into their phones, people who put down their wives when they're in public, people who order far too much food in Indian restaurants and waddle home, people who throw rubbish out of their car window, racists ... the list is endless.

Of course, there are obviously exceptions to every rule, and I do have to confess that I have thrown rubbish out my car window – but only apple cores. You see, my logic is that if you are on a rural road and you chuck an apple core out of the window, you could either feed a hungry mouse and her family, or at worst, it will decompose and do the environment some good. So one day, as I was travelling along a dual carriageway, I finished eating my apple and felt it was better to throw the core out of the passenger side, because if I threw it into the centre reservation the hungry mouse may get killed crossing the road. So I opened the passenger window (I could do that because I have a big expensive car and can open the passenger window with the touch of a button), and once the window was open, I projected the core in a kerbside direction hoping it would reach the undergrowth. Unfortunately, I hadn't opened the passenger window; I had opened the driver's window. And consequently, as I threw the core with great force, it splattered on the closed window and promptly bounced back at me, although now separated into 100 (approximately: I didn't actually count them) smaller pieces.

I'm sure there is a moral to this story, although I haven't worked out what it is.

But why are people like that?

Why is the child a bully? Is it to get attention because they don't get enough at home? Why do some men rape innocent girls? Is it because they themselves were abused as children? Why do husbands put down their wives in public? Is it because they themselves are constantly humiliated at work? Because of a bully? Who is seeking attention?

I don't know.

Basically, I'm guilty of judging at the point of contact, instead of trying to understand the person.

WE ARE ALL 'SOMEBODY'

I was staying in a moderately priced hotel at an African beach resort, enjoying a quiet drink by the pool with Sue. You could hear the gentle lapping of the waves and very little else. Suddenly, the peace was shattered by a gentleman from another part of the world, supposedly talking to his family, but addressing everybody within a half-mile radius,

We will have a party and it will be one hell of a party, and anybody who is somebody will be there.

As much as I didn't want to listen to this character it was unavoidable. I kept thinking to myself,

I bet the pool attendant won't be there, and he is somebody. And I bet the waiter won't be there, and he is somebody. In fact, I doubt I will be there, and I know that I am somebody.

So are we all 'somebody'? Somebody who, at our core, just wants to be loved, and when we don't get love, we have to demand it in other ways?

13

THE POVERTY PROBLEM

Let us turn our attention to why some African women have a large number of children, causing us in the West to say,

Well, if she can't feed them all, she shouldn't have them.

Let me introduce a poor African man – let's say he's a carpenter, and let's call him Darren. Darren comes along and meets a poor African girl – let's call her Joy. Darren meets Joy, Darren tells Joy he loves her, one thing leads to another and Joy becomes pregnant. On hearing that Joy is pregnant, Darren disappears, because he either can't afford, or doesn't want to afford, the cost of bringing up a child. So Darren's a pinhead.

But what about Joy? Why didn't she protect herself? Perhaps it is because some women gain their significance from having children? Why might she think like that?

Joy is one of 15 other children.

Joy wasn't sent to school and so can't gain a sense of significance through education.

Joy has no self-esteem.

And there are probably at least 10 more reasons which I am unaware of.

Joy now has 1, maybe 2, maybe 3 children. And each time, it is because a man has told her that he loves her; and each time, she prays that it is true; and each time, he legs it once he has got what he wants and is faced with responsibility.

So what does Joy have to do to survive? One of her options is to sell sex, because she knows there is plenty of demand for this. For a few quid a go, Joy can make some money to feed the family that Darren, or John or Rory should be helping to finance. We criticize Joy and take the moral high ground, horrified that a young mother, with young children, is selling sex behind the curtain separating her from her children in order to feed those children.

Then Joy gets HIV, and we feel some pity for her; but we also demand,

Why didn't you protect yourself?

But when it's a choice between a loaf of bread or a piece of protective rubber, and it's a case of 'either/or', what would you choose? So, instead, we ask Joy,

Why did you take the risk?

And Joy says,

If I don't sell sex, I'll have no money and I will definitely starve to death. If I do sell sex, I may become HIV positive, I may get aids and I may die. The odds are better selling sex than not selling sex.

So:

- you have a poor man who wants sex, but can't afford to support a child,
- you have a poor woman who desperately wants love and significance, and is prepared to take a risk,
- you have a young mother with no way of feeding her child,
- you have a prostitute,
- you have an AIDS victim who dies,
- you have 3 orphaned children,
- you have a grandmother left with the responsibility of bringing up 3 children,

- you have 3 children whose grandmother can't afford their education,
- you have 3 prostitutes in the making.

If you could change one thing
If you could change one reaction in the chain, what would be the impact?
- Give Joy a good education, then maybe Joy would find her only significance isn't in having children?
- Make condoms available for free, then maybe Joy wouldn't get pregnant and would be protected from other infections?
- Teach moral values so that Darren only has sex with Joy once they are married and they are committed to each other for life? (Only I think the Western world has led the way in demonstrating that's highly unlikely to work.)
- Establish an efficient welfare state, providing for as many children as Joy can produce, so that people could beat the system, sitting on their bottoms for the rest of their lives, dependent on handout after handout – but at least Joy wouldn't have to sell sex.

Or:

- Ensure Darren gets paid properly for being a carpenter, and ensure that Joy also has work that pays properly.

THINK ABOUT WHY

Part of the problem in Kenya is that business owners can get away with paying very low wages – not because there is no money in construction, but because of supply and demand. In Kenya, there is such a ready supply of unskilled or semi-skilled labour that wages are very low.

This is part of a wider problem, and when a supermarket chain sells 3 tailored shirts for £4 RRP, how much do you think anyone involved in the production of those shirts gets paid? When you are paying £2 for a cup of coffee in a coffee shop, think about the farmer, who probably only gets paid 40p per kilo – and that's even for a coffee that is billed as 'Fairtrade'. Where did the rest of the money go between the coffee shop and the farmer?

∿∿∿∿∿∿∿∿∿∿∿∿∿∿∿∿∿∿∿∿∿∿∿∿∿

Let's just pause there ...

Because you might think that I am against Fairtrade; I am certainly not. I know a business that sells dried fruit and that works with their supply chain to increase the farmers' yield and to promise a fair price at harvest time, when most people are trying to knock the price down. I can remember when Fairtrade goods only took up one shelf in the supermarket; now there are aisles and aisles of Fairtrade. In 2016, £158m was paid in premiums to Fairtrade producers around the world – that simply means you and I paying a tiny bit more to enhance the income of the producer.[4] So please don't stop buying Fairtrade; please do buy Fairtrade products. But you and I know we can always do more.

4 http://www.fairtrade.org.uk/What-is-Fairtrade/What-Fairtrade-does/Fairtrade-Premium (Accessed 27 March 2019).

Pause over!

~~~~~~

So next time you get off the plane from some beautiful beach resort, and the food and drinks and ice creams were so cheap, and you are telling your friends what a great holiday you had, and your nose is peeling from the sun, and you are laden with Duty Free goodies, and you have posted your favourite poolside photos of you drinking your 3rd cocktail of the day on Facebook and you tell your friends what a great resort it was, and that everything was so cheap ...

Think about why.

And in case you are struggling for an answer, it is so cheap because of the pathetic wages of:

- the farmers producing the food,
- the waiters serving you the food,
- the management looking after you,
- the cleaners making your bed,
- the gardener making your poolside look idyllic,
- the pool attendants saving you from catching killer diseases whilst swimming,
- the security guard protecting your fake watches that you buy from China, which are produced in a sweatshop in Beijing where workers are paid little more than 50p a day.

More equal than others

Basically, sometimes we are aware of our selfishness and lack of concern for the poor, and other times we are just downright ignorant. Both are surely inexcusable. Aren't they?

You see, the problem possibly is that we believe that we are all equal, it's just that some are more equal than others. And as much as we try to ignore it or deny it, our wealth does affect how people treat us. Therefore, money is not only important because it allows us to buy the essentials of life, but because it also creates our standing in society. You see, we are not all equal.

But surely, you might ask, don't we all start out as equal when we come out of the womb? Well no, not even there. I was born with a reasonably good brain and very good looks, I was born in a politically stable country, I had access to a fantastic education which enabled me to develop my brain – I even studied at university for free, which tells you how old I am! As a child, I never missed a meal or wondered whether I was going to get dinner that night; dinner was simply always there – it wasn't a miracle, it was life. Since reaching adulthood, I have never been out of work. I think I have only had one day off sick in my employed life, and even then I called the office only to find that nobody was there because the snow had been so heavy that everyone else had decided to stay home that day too.

But what if I had been born with a far more limited brain and ugly? What if the country I was born in was at war? What if my parents had to pay for my education and they couldn't afford it? What if university was completely unreachable? What if my dinner wasn't there every evening? What if employment was only running at 65%? Would my life be different?

Would it be different? It would be unrecognizable!

Do I have the right to look down on the poor, to dismiss the ugly, to scorn the single mum, to judge the prostitute, to wallow in my luxury, to be self-centred, to ignore the disadvantaged in order to consume my wealth and throw a few coins at the destitute?

I am not 'somebody' because I drive a Range Rover (which I don't). I'm not 'somebody' because I live in a nice house (which I do). I'm not 'somebody' because I'm a good public speaker (which I am). I'm not 'somebody' because I can afford to go to the Caribbean for my holiday (which I can). I'm not 'somebody' because I can fly first class (which I can't). I'm not 'somebody' because I eat in fancy restaurants (which I can). I'm not 'somebody' because I have a fat bank account (which I don't). I'm not 'somebody' because I have a yacht (which I don't). I know I have privilege, but that does not make me 'somebody'.

I am 'somebody' because God made me special. I am 'somebody' because God loves me. I am 'somebody' because when God made me, God thought,

Perfect: I'm not going to make another one like that!
I am 'somebody' because my wife loves me so much that she has given me the support to go and do things that most people can only dream about. I am 'somebody' because my friends have encouraged me to go for it.

We read in Colossians that there is no:

Gentile or Jew,
Circumcised or uncircumcised,
Barbarian, Scythian, slave or free ...[5]

I know you really shouldn't add to the Bible, because then it removes our understanding of the 'inspired word of God', but I am going to add a little more. There is no:

Rich or poor,
Male or female,
Land Cruiser driver or Corolla driver,
Lawyer or mason,
English or French,
Educated or uneducated,
Prostitute or pastor,
Catholic or Pentecostal,
Sophisticated or unsophisticated.

There is no wrong side of the tracks. And now back to the Bible: 'but Christ is all, and is in all'.

All that matters is Christ. Christ can live in anybody of any background, colour, tribe, race, family tree, class, language. All these are completely irrelevant to Christ. Whatever our natural or engineered differences, Christ unites us all by one Spirit into the unity of kingdom, where kingdom is God's purposes fulfilled on earth.

5 Colossians 3:11.

You see, my Bible teaches that we are all the same, but few of us really believe it – even the people who claim to live by the Bible's guidelines and rules. We are actually all the same, with different skills and abilities, but skills and abilities nonetheless. And just because my skill or ability might be better paid than yours, that doesn't make me any better than you.

AND THE ANSWER IS ...

Where does all this leave us? Because we still have pinheads in the world – and plenty of them – but we are the way we are for all kinds of reasons, most of which we never see. In all honesty, we probably can't do anything about it now. Because, regardless of everything I have just said, the majority of the world won't read this book (something I have to come to terms with), and even if some of the pinheads do read it – if *you* are one of those pinheads – your history, my history, is so ingrained that it is very, very hard to change.

But the truth is, I can do something about me. I can do something about my attitude, about my responses, about my ignorance, about my responsibility. Do I wear clothes that are made in a sweatshop in Beijing? I have absolutely no idea, but probably I do. Will I stop now that I have been made aware of it? I would love to, but I don't know how. OK, the 3 shirts for £4 are pretty obvious, but sometimes we can pay lots of cash for clothes made under the same conditions, and be completely unaware. How do I take a stand?

Do I judge the prostitute (I'm sure I have) or am I prepared to do anything to help her?

Can my attitude to other people change?

Can I own up to my responsibility?

Will I have compassion for the orphaned child?

Do I tip my waiters enough on holiday?

Will I buy Fairtrade?

Will I … ?

And the answer is,

I can do something.

SO DO WE REALLY CARE?

If I can't remember the root of my sense of injustice, I am aware of the things that fuelled it. Like the Rwandan slaughter in the nineties. At that time, as a family, we sponsored a Rwandan girl called Muja through her education. We had a standing order with our bank for £15 a month and at night, after we had told our children a bedtime story, we would pray and encourage the children to pray for Muja. We used to get letters from Muja once every 3 months and we received a new photo each year. Then the crisis came, and we lost touch with Muja for about a year and a half. We didn't know if she was alive or dead and,

Did we really care?

That sounds harsh; but I began to wonder whether, if we swapped Vicky (my daughter) with Muja, and if it was Vicky who lived in Rwanda whilst this genocide was happening, would we simply send £15 per month and pray? No, we would not. We would be trying everything we could think of to get her out of Rwanda; we would have been knocking on Margaret Thatcher's door, shouting about it, asking how we can, as a civilized nation, stand by and do nothing; we would have been campaigning for Vicky. To be honest, we probably wouldn't have slept at night and our efforts would have been completely focused on saving Vicky's life.

But what had Muja done to deserve being born in Rwanda, in an unstable country, dragged into a war which she knew nothing about? And what had Vicky done to deserve being born into a stable country, living in peace and harmony with not a worry in the world (at that age)? Answer:

Nothing.

Neither of them had done anything. As that slowly sunk in and I considered my own privileged life, which I had likewise done nothing to deserve, I had to conclude,

That's not fair.

But surely there is something I can do about it, and possibly we all get there at certain points in our thought processes, but conclude that the task is too big and ask what difference one individual can make. But what about the story of the little boy on the beach, who helped the starfish back into the sea so that they wouldn't die? He knew he wouldn't be able to save all of the starfish – that there were too many starfish for him to make any real difference. But he knew that he would make a difference to those starfish he *did* manage to save. There is something that we can do, but it's often a grain of sand in a desert of problems and it all feels so overwhelming.

But I can do something.

People react to injustice differently. Some get angry. Some write posts on Facebook. Some get politicized.

I started a charity: Hand in Hand.

~~~~~~

POINTS TO PONDER

- Never buy 3 shirts for £4; somebody is being exploited somewhere.
- Always tip the waiter generously; the likelihood is that they get paid significantly less than you.
- Never wear your sunglasses inside, you look ridiculous.
- Always remember everyone is somebody, and they might not be special to you, but they are always special to God.
- Never become a pinhead.

CHAPTER 2

THE ANSWER IS – I CAN DO SOMETHING

or

HOW I STARTED A CHARITY

GO THERE THEN

I have a friend called Pete. One evening, about 30 years ago, Pete rang me to say that he was going as part of a group on a 'mercy mission' to Romania: would I like to go?

My answer was,

No.

Why not? Pete asked.

I responded,

Everyone is going to Romania at the moment, I'm not jumping on the 'bandwagon'.

Pete asked what else I was doing at that time to help people.

Nothing much, I replied.

Then why don't you do something and come to Romania?

It seemed a fair enough argument, and so I went. Incidentally, I recall coming home from that visit in my socks, because Pete had given my trainers away.

I have another friend: Dave. Dave had visited an education project in the Brazilian city of Fortaleza. Dave became inspired. Subsequently, Dave brought Pete to the project and Pete, too, became inspired. The two of them began to raise money for the project unofficially, through various fundraising events including a sponsored cycle across the UK. Then, 10 years after the 'Romanian' phone call, Pete rings me again,

Dave and I would like to register a charity. You know how charities work; we need to have 3 trustees; so will you join us so we can register Hand in Hand as an official charity?

At that time, I was a volunteer consultant for another charity called Tearfund (a charity whose Christian response to poverty I really believe in). My consultancy, however, specialized in the development of theological colleges in East Africa; for Pete and Dave to suggest that I knew how charities operate was a bit like saying that I understand how aeroplanes work simply because I had flown in one. Regardless of Pete's logic, my answer was, again,

No.

After the Romanian experience, I probably should have known better. I am sure you can guess Pete's next question:

Why not?

Because we already have some great charities that are doing a great job, like Tearfund, World Vision and Christian Aid. etc. What is the point in reinventing the wheel? We should support these existing charities.

Not at all put off by my response and knowing how easily I change my mind, Pete then said,

Go there then.

Go where? I asked.

To Brazil. Go to Fortaleza and see the project, then make your decision.

Pete has a way with words, and this seemed like a fair challenge. So I went.

Because he cared

I met a man called Marcondes. Marcondes was a local, was well-educated and had the potential to be a wealthy man. But he had given his life to helping some 300 children who lived in a slum close to him. Within this slum he had created an oasis of security and support, giving poor children the opportunity to have a fair start in life.

I will never forget that trip and what I saw there, yet it's difficult to put into words. Here was an educated man who could have been very wealthy, but had given his life to help 300 children from the favela. He said his ambition had always been to build a 50m swimming pool in the slum. I asked,

What for?

And he said,

Because a poor kid can swim just as fast as a rich kid, and I want to give them the opportunity.

Some people give to charity because it makes them feel better. It makes them feel better about injustice – it makes them feel like they are doing something, and perhaps that is what we were doing by sponsoring Muja. But some people do it because they genuinely care.

Nelson Mandela was a man with a story like Marcondes: he was well educated, held a good job and was financially stable. Yes – as a black man he faced the injustice of apartheid, but when he fought, it wasn't for the improvement of his own bank account or his own situation; he was fighting for others. He was fighting because of the injustice that meant the black population was treated in such a degrading way that the majority couldn't get good jobs, couldn't afford food and were forced to live in slums. Mandela's fight was not to lift his own life out of poverty, but to change the lives of millions who were crippled by it. And to achieve this change he suffered in prison at the hands of the 'justice' system for a large proportion of his life.

How often do we hear of people raising money for cancer research because they or a family member have lived through the trauma of cancer? How many times do we hear of people fighting for road safety because their child was run over outside the school gate, or campaigning for a gun amnesty because their child was shot? When there is a personal connection, when they have been personally affected, people care.

Marcondes did not need to run a children's home for the benefit of his own income, he did not fight poverty because he was brought up in poverty, he did not offer a good education to children because he was uneducated; he did it because he cared. He did it out of love. And as a consequence of his selfless love, he was loved. It was all about love. Not a distant, duty-bound response to poverty, but the giving something of yourself, getting involved and allowing yourself to be affected. Marcondes was an inspiration for me. I returned home, and Hand in Hand was registered.

BECOMING AN INTERNATIONAL
JUMPER IMPORTER

Remember, at this time, I was volunteering for Tearfund, and also with a youth ministry group called Viz-A-Viz that challenged young people to respond to poverty. Through Viz-A-Viz, we took a youth team to see 2 Tearfund projects on the outskirts of Nairobi. At the end of the 2 weeks, 3 of the lads – Jon, Jon and Dan – said that they would like to raise money for one of the projects. During the trip we had visited a church project that provided wool for poor women in the community to knit jumpers which the church then sold to provide income for these women. I know what you're thinking: jumpers? In Africa? Have they really got the right market? Well, it does sometimes get cold in Kenya, but not so cold that the church had sold out of jumpers – in fact they probably had about 500 surplus.

Jon, Jon and Dan wanted to buy 100 jumpers to sell in the UK. (Easier said than done!) Five jumpers could probably be squeezed into your suitcase, 10 jumpers might require you to buy an extra bag. But 100? After a little research, it became apparent that we effectively had to become an importer. I offered that Hand in Hand would import the jumpers and pay for them, then the 3 lads would pay us back. From memory, we needed about £2,200 to pay for the jumpers and freight them. As you may guess, neither HiH nor I had the cash to finance this, but I knew a friend who would – and he did. I won't bore you with the details, but suffice to say that one day, some cardboard boxes of jumpers arrived at our house. As luck would have it, there were 3 boxes: one for each of the 3 young men wanting to sell them.

Jon, Jon and Dan started to sell the jumpers. If I'm being completely honest, these jumpers could have been the best jumpers you had ever bought ... if you had one arm slightly longer than the other and were a bit colour blind. However, most people have equi-length arms and can distinguish colours quite happily. Yet nearly all of the jumpers were bought! The truth is, most sales made were probably due more to the buyers wanting to support the lads and their desire to help, rather than their desire to make a fashion statement. Having said that, one guy I know still proudly wears his Kenyan jumper like it's the best jumper he ever bought!

For me, it just seemed logical to support the lads in their desire to help the poor and import the jumpers. (Possibly the mistake was bringing in 100 and not 10, but it was the lads' idea and I went along with it!) But the jumpers sold, and you will read about the trickle-down effect of their efforts in the pages ahead. Two thirds of the jumper trio have since become trustees of Hand in Hand, and Jon H went on to work for Ambassadors in Sport and is still ministering through sport today, inspired by his visit to Kenya.

This is how Hand in Hand began in Africa, and today it supports 3,000 children year after year. Would all of that have happened without the jumpers? I can't actually say, but those 100 oddly-shaped pullovers have had a significant impact on so many people's lives. Sometimes you have to go with your gut, fly by the seat of your pants and trust that God can pull it out the bag. And all I can say is that sometimes it works, and sometimes it doesn't. On this occasion it worked.

That is how the charity began.

IT COSTS MORE THAN MONEY

Most people don't believe this next bit, but it's true. Sue and I have never had money. Don't misunderstand me: I am not pretending to be poor – we enjoy a very nice lifestyle, but I only ever worked part time, we have never saved and we have no investments. Our attitude could have been:

Let's work 6 days a week and give 3 days' money to Hand in Hand.

I was probably earning around £350 per day, so that would mean giving the charity £1,000 per week and £50k per year. You can do a lot with £50k and, believe me, there have been many times when I have thought that this would have been a really good way to contribute.

But the problem with the model is that I know my own nature: I would never have given £1,000 per week. And even if, by some miracle, I was disciplined and routinely gave the required amount, the danger was that without a sense of connection and responsibility to the project, these donations would likely have become just another transaction to make me feel better. Ultimately, I decided that it was my time that I should be giving, and my consultancy work could be used to fund my flights and to help build networks. I never did work those 6 days a week, choosing instead to do 2 or 3, giving my time to the development of HiH. As I write this book now, the income of Hand in Hand and the investment of the business amount to way beyond what £1,000 a week could have achieved. It was worth my putting in the time, but it remained something that we debated amongst ourselves for a long while.

Within a few years of registering the charity, Sue, Jon and Dan had become trustees and we were managing to raise £30k per year through fundraising events and the generosity of friends. The philosophy, very much gleaned from the good practice and principles that I had learned though working with Tearfund, was that Hand in Hand would support what local Christians were already doing in their response to poor communities around them. Clearly, Brazilians and Kenyans know far better than folk from the UK about what the most appropriate response to poverty in their own communities is. In 20 years, this basic philosophy hasn't changed. We raise money in the UK and Kenya to support what local people are doing in order to alleviate poverty in their communities.

AND SO WE ARE DOING SOMETHING

We are doing something for Jennifer, whose daughter – let's call her Julie – died of HIV last year. Jennifer farms a dry ribbon of land in order to feed her 11 grandchildren. When the rains failed and she couldn't pay the water bill, her water was disconnected, the ground dried out and cracked, there was nothing for breakfast and she constantly worried about how she would feed her grandchildren. So Hand in Hand fixed new guttering to her roof and gave her a rainwater barrel so that water is collected whenever it rains. They have paid her water bill, so the supply is re-connected. They have given her a drip kit,[6] so now her crops are watered in

6 A simple and highly efficient irrigation mechanism: a hose with narrow holes at intervals which means that only the roots of the plants are watered and evaporation is kept to a minimum.

the most efficient way possible. And now there is almost always breakfast for Jennifer's grandchildren.

We are doing something for the 300 or so children and the handful of mothers and babies at New Hope Children's Home. Mothers like Jasmine – a teenager who came to the door with her twins a year previously, weak and exhausted. They were just 1 month old, but she asked if she could leave one child with us because she did not have enough milk for both; she could not cope. Perhaps the stronger one? He would have a better chance. Anne – a retired Kenyan bank manager who, along with her husband, had always wanted a big family (be careful what you pray for) and who the 300 or so now all call 'Mum' – welcomed Jasmine, explaining that there was another way: she could stay, and with both of her babies. So Jasmine stayed in the mother and baby room with about 6 other young teenage mums, some of whom were studying and some who were helping to look after the toddlers. Jasmine fed both her babies and is now studying hairdressing at a nearby college while her twins play in the toddlers' room, looked after by the volunteer nurses.

We are doing something for children like Daniel. He is one of the 300 or so who sleep in the spotless but simple dormitories at New Hope, who wear mismatched clothing and play football outside on the grass after school and after dinner. And yes, there is dinner every night – it's a miracle, and it's life – every night there is dinner.

However, if you press her, Anne will tell you that there was one night, 17 years ago, when the girls on kitchen duty came to her and said that there was nothing left: no more food and no more maize for the flour to make Ugali.[7] So Anne said,

> *Still put the water on to boil in the kitchen; the Lord will provide.*

So the girls put the enormous pans of water on to boil – it took some time as they were very large. Anne prayed,

> *Lord, these are your children. I'm not going to send them to bed hungry. Please would you send food for them.*

And just as the water was beginning to boil, there was a knock on the door. A nearby school was going away on a trip for the holidays and had not wanted to waste their leftover food. They knew there was an orphanage nearby and determined to find it. They brought sacks of maize flour and oil, and the children all ate well that night.

We are doing something for Janice, who was brought to New Hope; her father was missing, her mother couldn't cope. Janice came, and was loved and was fed and was educated. Janice went on to study at university, and today she and her husband are both police inspectors, and they have children who could also become police inspectors one day, if they wanted to.

Now, the police force in Kenya doesn't have the best reputation; in fact, more often than not when someone gets arrested, it tends to be the police who are up to mischief rather than the accused. One day, one of my staff was being threatened with arrest due to spurious accusations, and so I telephoned Janice (her ringtone is a Christian song). I got through to her voicemail and left a message. Then 10 minutes later she called back: the police officer in question had already been dealt with and if ever I had a problem like

7 A type of cornmeal porridge made in Africa.

this again, all I needed to do was call her. I ask her,

How can you have a Christian ringtone working for the police in Kenya?

And Janice tells me,

Mum (she means Anne) always taught us to trust God and to do the right thing. Yes – I am in the police force, and a lot of people don't like me, but I still trust God and do the right thing.

We are doing something for Derek, who was brought up in a loving family, but who was just too poor. When he gets to secondary school age his family can't afford the fees. He goes to New Hope and asks if it might be possible for them to pay his school fees for him, and they do. Derek excels and decides he would like to train as a nurse. HiH sponsor his fees once more, and once more Derek excels, studying for 4 years and qualifying as a nurse. But he wants to go further, so he gets a job as a nurse and manages to pay for his own training as an anaesthetist. Today, Derek currently sponsors 3 children through education and wants to open his own children's home to show his thanks to the home that loved him.

One way or another, around 3,000 Daniels and Dereks, and Janices, and Jennifers and Jasmines are helped by Hand in Hand.

Which is something.

It is definitely something.

And we are thankful.

But ...

The trouble with charities is there are so many of them, all with their begging bowl out. Every time we ask people to support Hand in Hand financially, we become acutely aware that there are so many pressures on people's spending, and that there are thousands of great charities that are doing good work – many in the same way as us. Why should people support our ideas any more than anyone else's?

I ask myself,

Is there another way to raise money and have an even bigger impact?

My answer is,

Yes.

CHAPTER 3

WE ARE DOING EVERYTHING WE CAN

or

WHY I STARTED A BUSINESS

Some of you out there might be doubters and might think that charities and NGOs are more self-serving than serving their purpose. In the 20 years that HiH charity has been in existence, I have never taken a penny in salary, expenses, gifts in kind – nothing. You may detect a little irritation in that statement, and you would be right, because it has been insinuated that I *do* live off the back of the charity. I certainly have not and do not. My income has come from consulting as a quantity surveyor and through the HiH *business* activities in both the UK and Kenya – but never from the charity.

Just had to get that off my chest!

QUANTITY SURVEYORS COUNT

I was not born a businessman. I was not trained to be a businessman. But through the events and circumstances of life, I somehow became a businessman. I started my working life as a quantity surveyor. Most of you might not know what a QS does, but it was fully explained at my graduation – a hot, stuffy affair where we were addressed by a Fellow of the Royal Institute of Chartered Surveyors. He said that quantity surveyors were very similar to rhinos, because we are very thick-skinned and charge a lot.

What we do is count things. And we count the cost of them. I tend to count everything: number of steps to walk into town; number of steps on a staircase (which, by the way, is usually 13–15); number of floor tiles until I get to the check-in counter at the airport; number of people on the bus; I'll even count the number of people at a concert or a football match, which is actually much easier than you might think. You'll be glad to know that I have never counted the number of peas on the plate, or the number of cars on the motorway (although I do count the number of Eddie Stobart lorries on a journey). As a QS, the point of your count is to value something fairly – I would always work to pay the contractor fairly; I wouldn't want to be clever and pay him less than the true value of the work, neither would I want to pay him more.

As a QS, I always tried to be fair. It is likely that this sense of fairness in my work was motivated by the same attitude that fuelled my hatred for injustice. When you take time to dwell on injustice in the world, you end up getting stuck between a rock and a hard place. Because, if you're truly honest with yourself, there is little benefit in pointing the finger at others, asking them what more they could do; instead you are forced to start looking at yourself – to ask what more *you* could do.

And you start counting, you start comparing and contrasting: that nice meal out compared to the difference that money could have made to 1 child whose education it could have funded for 6 months; or the amount I spend on a holiday which could fund construction at the orphanage; or if we cut £20 from our food bill per month, which is quite doable and we certainly wouldn't starve, that £20 could sponsor another child; and if I bought cheaper shoes (I could buy something out of the Charity Christmas gift catalogue); or if we only had 1 car and I cycled more (not only would it do me good, the environment good, the parking in our street good, it could contribute towards another salary to work with the charity).

Basically, for every damn thing I spend my money on, there is a cheaper alternative, and I could do better things with the savings, and hey, I have a choice; but there are so many people who will wake up tomorrow to no breakfast because they have no choice, because there is no breakfast to have, because they used their last flour, or maize, or milk or bread the night before.

So I argue with myself that I don't live a lavish life style, that leather shoes are more economical because they last longer, that I need to have a holiday to prevent burn out and that if I don't take Sue out to dinner, I may have no marriage.

But now just let me explain that to Mary who has been left with 6 grandchildren to bring up at the age of 70, when she should be sitting on her porch step, chatting to other grandmothers, enjoying her grandchildren at weekends and giving them back when they are getting tiring. But no, she has got to milk the cow if she is lucky enough to have one, and sell vegetables in the market if there has been a crop, and wash the kids' clothes, because her daughter, their mother, died of malnutrition.

So I live with all these tensions.

~~~~~~~~~~~~~~~~~~~~~~~~

EVERYTHING WE CAN...?

On my first visit to Kenya, I went with a youth team, as I mentioned in the last chapter. We slept on classroom floors, not because the teachers were so boring that we fell asleep – these were the sleeping arrangements. We dug foundations for a hairdressing salon and we played with Lucy, and Mikey, and Daniel and Janet, and yep, that changes everything. Suddenly you know real children instead of nameless pictures on the underground or on TV. Part of the trip included my first visit to a slum house. I say 'house' – in truth, it was a corrugated iron structure that had 1 room divided by a curtain, no sewage, no electricity, no water, no dignity, really. Then you start to understand that these allotment sheds – which is really all they are – are actually owned by somebody who charges these people rent.

So we go into this little home – that's what it is to this family – and there are a few pots and pans; a bed which the whole family sleep in; a bowl for washing the dishes, and washing the children, and peeling the veg and washing the clothes ... and some washed clothes and a bench to sit on, which is probably borrowed because Mary knew we were coming, and it's all dark because there are no windows and no lights, and the smell of smoke because they are cooking something on a fire just outside. You start thinking: what happens when it rains or it's cold, because even in Africa it can rain and it can get cold. How would you get anything dry when you come in from the rain and the mud, clothes soaking wet, and your entire home is also damp? It just leaves you helpless.

Our team of 10 all cram into this grandmother's room, and in the darkness you can pick out the frame of a thin, frail woman who is clearly sick: no need for a gym membership for her so that she can lose those excess pounds put on at Christmas. We are all a bit overcome by the situation, trying to make conversation. Then the person who brought us puts one of the team on the spot and says,

Will you pray for this lady?

What do you say? What do you pray? Where is God at that point in that desperate situation? So the person on the spot said before he prayed,

I just want you to know that we are doing everything we can back in the UK to help you.

As we all listened to his words, we all knew that it was a lie: we all knew we were not doing 'everything we could'.

Not the spokesperson's fault, he was put on the spot, and I doubt any of us would have said anything better. He was only trying to show her that we cared – and we did care, but not to that extent.

This story is bad enough. But then, a few months later, the story is retold to a group of people and much the same point was added, that obviously we knew that statement wasn't true, but he goes and makes it worse. How does he make it worse? Because he adds,

But one day, I want to go back to that lady when that statement is true, and admit that whilst it wasn't true then, it is now.

Oh great, so how are you going to do that then? That just ain't going to happen. Why is that not going to happen?

1. She's dead now.
2. We aren't even scratching the surface of 'everything we could' do.
3. Who even is 'we'?
4. Forget the 'we', what about just *me*? Am I ever going to be doing everything *I* could do?

So why is that a worse statement? Because the first one was just a downright lie, the second is within our ability: we can try and get a bit closer to doing everything that we can. But we can try until we die, and we will still miss the mark by miles. Still – he has raised the challenge to try, which we shouldn't turn our back on.

It was Jon (real name, identity preserved) who made this challenge: the Jon who became a trustee of HiH charity and who is doing a lot to rectify the first statement. But, the statement will never become true, will it?

So we have started a charity, we support some local partners supporting orphanages and schooling and grand-mothers' projects, and we help maybe 3,000 people. And that is something.

But it is not:

Everything we can.

MORE THAN A DELAYING TACTIC?

There are approximately 2.5m people living in the slum in Nairobi. Which is over 60% of the total population of the city.[8] And there are loads of self-effacing charities that are doing great work and are committed to the causes they are passionate about. There are charities which have changed people's lives; charities that have had an impact long after the point of contact; charities that have helped children into education who have ended up going to university and finding a career, getting married and having 2.2 children and supporting their own parents. There are loads of great stories like that, and I could talk of so many specific examples of children supported by Hand in Hand that have gone on to support themselves long after we stepped back.

But I start to think,

What next?

In charity work, you have to think like that because:

- the donor money could run out,
- there is more demand than donor money can support.

8 Kibera Facts & Information, https://www.kibera.org.uk/facts-info/(Accessed 4 February 2019).

And anyway, how can we be sure we are making a lasting difference?

When we support a child through education, does it give them the foundation to maximize their potential, or are we just making ourselves feel good, but ultimately only delaying the cycle of poverty so that these supported children will end up back where they came from, only now they have an education? Great!

As I wrestle with all of this in my mind, I start to think, *Can we actually create sustainable jobs and careers that are properly paid and that offer a reasonable standard of living, rather than just a delaying tactic, putting off the onset of poverty?*

And ultimately, that leads you to business.

Beyond bracelets and wood carvings

You see, many charitable organizations have been involved in businesses: cottage industries, Fairtrade, Traidcraft, Microfinance, etc. This is all very well, and they provide real support for the entrepreneurial types who have initiative, who can cope with their own informal business, who are happy to manage cash flow; many of these initiatives work. But they have their downsides: there are only so many bracelets you can wear at once; there are only so many carvings you can fit around one fireplace. And how fair, really, are the Fairtrade groups who have now created their own monopoly and have to be bribed to pay you the Fairtrade price for your coffee?[9] And how many people in poverty can keep repaying the Microfinance in order to actually remain in business for more than a season or two?

9 Not the fault of the organization, but the weakness of the implementation. And so, as I said before, please don't stop buying Fairtrade, or things will just get worse.

Am I saying that all of the above is a waste of time? Certainly not – it works for many, but it also doesn't work for many. Some people can't cope with managing a business, some people worry themselves sick that they owe £5 to the savings and loans community, and they only have £4. Some people just want to go to work, earn a fair day's pay, get paid at the end of the week and sleep easy.

Where are the charities creating those employment opportunities? As I looked around, there didn't seem to be so many.

So, I suggest to myself, let's start a business that employs lots of people and that pays above the minimum wage, so that the workers can support their families, without all the stress of running a small business. And let's do it profitably so that there is more than a single bottom line, but potentially a double or treble or quadruple bottom line, one that includes:

- Profit. Or financial responsibility. There has to be profit otherwise we are bankrupt, however, this profit should not only benefit the company, but should feed back into the charity so that we are not solely dependent on the continued goodwill of our supporters.
- Social responsibility. We need to structure our employment criteria to benefit all who contribute to the wealth of the business and to contribute to the redistribution of wealth in the nation.
- Environmental responsibility. We need to be mindful of our natural habitat and support it, rather than destroy it.

- Spiritual responsibility. We need to recognize the value of an individual, rather than treat them like a commodity.

THE PUB ECONOMIST'S PERSPECTIVE

I studied economics at A level. My teacher described me as a good 'pub' economist (an interesting choice of term for someone who was not yet 18, and therefore not legally allowed to set foot in a pub). What he meant was that I could articulate my understanding well, but struggled when it came to putting it on paper. Was he telling me that I had no future in economics, or, rather, that my economic future would have to wait for me to turn 18? Anyway, that aside, permit me to attempt to explain some basic economics in an industry that I do understand: construction. If you end up being more confused at the end of it, I suggest you invite me to a pub and I will explain it to you there!

A developer has 4 basic costs:

- Land
- Materials
- Finance
- People.

The land cost is dictated by the market and contributes to the calculation of the selling price of whatever you choose to build on that land. Materials are a relatively fixed cost, which is impacted by inflation. Finance is calculated by the rate and time of borrowings. The rest of the developer's cost is people.

In Kenya, construction workers such as masons, electricians and carpenters (like Darren) get paid in the region of £2 to £10 per day. The developer gets paid what he doesn't pay the construction workers who are creating the wealth. The developer could take home upward of £1,000 per day. Clearly I am over-simplifying here – it's a 'Grantism', if you like – but you get my point. The developer drives a Land Cruiser and lives in an exclusive 7-bedroom villa, whilst the construction worker lives in a tin shed and rides a bike, if he is lucky enough even to have the bike. I am not a communist, but this can't be right. My point is that construction workers are paid so poorly, not because there are no profit margins in construction, but because the professionals and the developer are paid disproportionately well.

Let's look at Darren again …

Darren is a carpenter fixing skirting boards, building wardrobes and installing kitchens on a housing estate of 300 houses in Nairobi. The houses sell for £75k, the income to the project is £22.5m. The workforce is made up of:

- Unskilled labour (Simon)
- Skilled labour (Darren)
- Professionals (Rebecca)
- Developer (Robert).

In Kenya, the unskilled labourer (Simon) will be paid £2.50 per day, the skilled labourer (Darren) will get paid £5 per day, the professional consultant (Rebecca) could get paid around £250 a day and the developer (Robert) gets paid whatever is left. (He will be aiming to be paid more than the professionals, however, otherwise he would become a professional!)

Fundamentally, Robert gets paid what he doesn't pay everyone else. Now I could get accused of over-simplification here, but the conclusion I come to is that Robert drives a Land Cruiser and lives in the mansion on the hill – which Darren's skills have effectively paid for – whilst Darren lives in a hole made of crinkly tin, with no sewage system, electricity or water.

You may question all this, but that is how the construction business works. I am not talking about how politicians get paid, or charity workers, or clergy, or teachers or civil servants; I am explaining the economics of how the construction business works. Basically – as I learned in my school economics class – supply and demand creates the price, and I suppose that there is just such a large available labour force in Kenya that the supply curve creates the low rates. Why construction workers don't get together and demand higher pay, I am not sure.

Now explain to me how this can be right? To me, morally, this is an abuse of power. And to someone who calls themself a Christian? Well somehow I can't get away from the idea that it must be abhorrent to God.[10] This is not only abhorrent to Darren and Simon; it is abhorrent to God. It is completely unjustifiable selfishness of the highest order, ignorance at best and downright evil at worst.

10 For a quick Bible study on this, I'd suggest the following verses as a starting point: Exodus 2:23–25; Leviticus 19:13; Deuteronomy 24:14–15; Psalm 10; Jeremiah 22:13; 1 Timothy 5:18; James 5:1–6.

And who creates the value? Without Darren and Simon there are no houses to sell for £75k. But they are building houses that they can only ever hope to work in. For Darren to talk of *owning* a house like the one he is building – well, that is like saying I am going to the moon for lunch. Maybe if Darren was paid properly, he could support his family. (Although I am not saying that is solely a male prerogative.) Maybe if Darren was paid properly he could pay school fees for his children instead of looking for donors to educate them, and maybe if Darren was paid properly he and his family could enjoy living in a £75k house and maybe if Darren was paid properly he too could drive his children to school in a Land Cruiser (if he wanted to).

And before you start thinking,

Glad I am not a developer in Kenya. What are those people over there going to do about it?

You may be surprised to hear that this example of business creating poverty is only one among many.

In the UK, at the time of writing, a QS can earn around £500 per day; with the lack of supply of quality masons, a mason can earn as much as a well-paid QS. I am no mathematician, but the gap in the UK between the construction worker and the professional has become very narrow, and potentially it could swing the other way. In Kenya the difference can be a hundredfold and more.

And, as I think all that, I am left with another set of questions:

- Can a commercial company do all that my business model suggests?

- Will any investor invest in such a company, given that potentially there are lower financial returns, but higher social benefits?
- Why am I not aware of anybody else doing it; does that suggest it can't work?
- What sort of business could we get involved in?

With all these questions largely unanswered I nevertheless become increasingly convinced that business is the right way to go – although it has to be in addition to the charity, not in place of it. Because, at the end of the day, you can't say to an orphaned child, or to a grandmother,

We won't feed you or pay for your grandchild's education, but we can offer you a job in our factory!

And so Hand in Hand Trading Ltd (HiHT)[11] begins; trading in what, I don't know; trading with who, I don't know; trading where, I don't know; importing or exporting, I don't know; with capital from where, I don't know. I am a quantity surveyor for goodness sake, how am I meant to know all these answers? But clearly business has a contribution to make to the poverty problem. The fact that I didn't know all the answers really didn't seem that important.

---

11 HiHT was renamed in 2016 and is now called HiHG (HiHGroup). More information on the structure of HiH can be found in the appendix.

~~~~~~~~~~~~~~~~~~~~~~~~~~~~~~~~~~~~~~

POINTS TO PONDER

- Business has an important contribution to make, in both creating poverty, and in alleviating it.
- When someone says they are doing 'all they can' they rarely are doing 'all they can'.
- Quantity surveyors count.

CHAPTER 4

SO WHAT MAKES A GOOD BUSINESS?

In the early nineties, Sue and I invested in some property in the UK and abroad. Shortly after we had made these investments, the property market crashed in the UK and interest rates trebled. After 5 years and some financial support from friends, we sold the properties and lost in the region of £100k (you will learn more about this later). Was this a successful business venture? I would say, by almost any measure, *no*. Had we done it perhaps 10 years later or 10 years earlier, our profit margin could have been completely different. But would that make it good? Can 'good' business be measured by financial output alone?

What I would like us to think about in this chapter is: what *really* is 'good' in terms of business? Fundamentally, most people understand 'good business' primarily in terms of money – profit, growth, the bottom line – however you want to phrase it, the terms are financial. A good business makes money. A very good business makes a lot of money.

Most people go into business because they want to make money – they believe they can deliver a product or service and make a profit from doing so. So, say I manufacture clothing: I win the contract to produce a well-known brand of jeans, and, because of the brand name, they command a high price and I make 300% profit on every pair of jeans. That sounds like a very good business. But then you find out that I pay my workers $1 a day and bribe import officials to avoid government duties. So is it *really* good? And *who* is it good *for*?

In fact, whenever you try to think of examples of 'good' businesses, there will generally be a down side, a 'cost'. Sports Direct are a profitable business, but have been criticized for their employment criteria, low rates of pay and bullying in the workplace.[12] IKEA sell furniture very cheaply – they are good value for money – because of the repeat designs, simplicity, economies of scale and reduced delivery cost for the business and for the customer. You just pick up the box and put it in your reasonably sized car. And lots of people do. This means, however, that you may find your neighbour has the same furniture as you and that you need an aptitude in puzzle solving in order to construct your latest purchase. And those are both costs. But it's hard to deny that IKEA is a successful business.

The supermarket chain Aldi are profitable, and their prices are extremely competitive, but the service is not as personal as if you went to a local butcher or grocer. In fact, you might say that any chain of superstores constitutes a successful business, almost by definition, but generally this

12 Simon Goodley and Jonathan Ashby, 'Revealed: how Sports Direct effectively pays below minimum wage', *The Guardian Online*, 9 December 2015, www.theguardian.com/business/2015/dec/09/how-sports-direct-effectively-pays-below-minimum-wage-pay.

comes at the cost of convenience and service, as well as a lot of other things. This description from Mark Greene's *The Best Idea in the World* describes some of them:

I grew up in a little suburb called Northwood on the edge of Greater London. From the age of about ten, my mum would send me down to the shops with money, a list and a pencil to write down what I'd paid. I'd go and see Mr Allen, the grocer, who was always happy and always knocked a few pennies off the bill, and then on to Mr Worbouys, who looked like a proper butcher, burly and ruddy-jowled and a little bit fearsome. They'd know my name and ask after my mum, and then I'd pop into Carey's to buy eight nails and put it on Mr Greene's account. But now, thirty years later, I have to get in the car, drive four miles, get stuck in the ring road traffic round Watford to have the deep joy of going into some hardware hypermarket called Seek & Queue on the off chance that they might actually have what I want, to be greeted by no one at all, and then scurry round the aisles like a blindfolded toddler in Hampton Court maze, chasing the always receding figure of a salesperson I have never met and who not only doesn't know my name but doesn't know my mother's name either. Only to discover that they don't have what I'm looking for, but that Nails R Us might – which requires another trip round the ring road. And this, I'm told, is progress.

Nevertheless, in the decade or so after leaving home, I'd go back into town and there'd still be people I knew and who would know me and ask after my mum. There was something warming about that continuity of relationship, about there being people you knew and who knew you, even if not necessarily very well, people you felt a definite affection for. But all those shops have closed now, and when I go to the supermarket, the people on the checkout seem to be different every time and they don't know my name and no one ever takes a few pennies off the bill. Computers don't work that way. Something's been lost.

How arid so many of our sorties into the world now seem. No wonder so many people shop online.[13]

The business examples we've named are all successful – they make money – but at what cost? To their workforce? To the customer, in terms of quality or service? To the environment or wider community? What seems 'good' to the Chief Executive or the shareholders may not seem so 'good' to the sales assistant who has to police the miles of aisles, or the scurrying customer in search of a bag of nails or the neighbour trying to tend their garden across from what is now a major ring road. Generally speaking, a company that is purely focused on the bottom financial line may have to sacrifice quality, service or price in order to deliver, and there will generally be an additional unseen cost to others.

However, here are some alternative examples to think about:

13 Mark Greene, *Probably the Best Idea in the World,* (Muddy Pearl: 2018), pp.43–44.

- Jesse Boot recognized that poor people couldn't access medication, and that the unit cost didn't warrant the high prices being charged. So he opened, effectively, the medicine supermarket, making medication affordable to those with a lower income. He saw an opportunity to make money *and* make medicine more accessible. Who knows how many people benefited from pain relief, antihistamines and cough syrup, how many people lived more comfortable lives or lived longer as a consequence of his company, Boots?[14]

- In 1920, Guinness workers had full medical and dental care, subsidized meals, company funded pensions, subsidized funeral expenses, education benefits, sports facilities and were given two pints of Guinness a day. In World War I, for each one of their employees who signed up to the army, Guinness paid half their salary directly to their family. In addition to all this, Guinness founded the first Sunday schools in Ireland, recognizing the importance of access to education for all. There were many other social firsts and achievements by Guinness. Today, Guinness is now brewed in 49 different countries and sold in over 150.[15] But as one review put it, *The Guinness tale is not primarily about beer. It is not even primarily about the Guinnesses. It is about what God can do with a person who is willing and with a corporation committed to doing something noble and good in the world.*[16]

14 Ian Bradley, *Enlightened Entrepreneurs: Business Ethics in Victorian Britain* (Lion Hudson: 2007), pp. 161–162.

15 Stephen Mansfield, *The Search for God and Guinness: A Biography of the Beer that Changed the World*, (Thomas Nelson: 2009), p. xxvii.

16 'The Story of God and Guinness: How the faith of Arthur Guinness inspired vision for his famous beer', *Relevant Magazine*, 25 March 2010.

- John Laing, a building contractor which was a household name after World War II and for the remainder of the century, had a reputation for quality and instigating many measures to make life better for those he employed. Laings were market leaders in the UK, among the first to introduce target-related pay, holiday pay and sick pay, alongside other employee benefits

Was he profitable? Certainly he was, although by the time he died, he had given all the money away or put it into trusts, which are still supporting charitable causes to this day.

Close to my own heart, Laings was a pioneer in employing (and developing the profession of) quantity surveyors (thank you John). His purpose for introducing this new role was to achieve accurate estimates for his clients. It so often happened that building contracts would go over budget because the estimates of work to be undertaken were not carried out thoroughly before construction commenced, resulting in legitimate additional cost to the client. With proper attention given to estimating, using the skills of quantity surveyors, these costs would be identified at pre-construction budget stage. This was so important, enabling the client to finance the construction from start to finish, rather than finding out close to the end that, actually, the budget was expended. This then led to the need for formal qualifications which, in turn, led to the Institute of Chartered Surveyors (ICS) in 1941 achieving professional recognition for the contractors. The ICS later merged with the Royal Institute of

Chartered Surveyors (RICS), still active today.[17] (As you can see, I really like quantity surveyors!)

I think we can see that the description of 'good' as applied to business can have wide and varied meanings, and is not necessarily purely financial. At the same time, there is a common assumption that only charities funded by donors can achieve social good. But, as the above examples illustrate, Boots, Guinness and Laing all made a valuable contribution to society, *and* made money doing it.

In my view, good business, like good work, is not *only* about making money. It is about creating value. Doing something which contributes to the well-being of ourselves and others.[18]

ONE SMALL STEP FOR HiH

It was Christmas and we were in our first year of building houses in Nairobi. We hadn't actually made any money at this point. We deliberated in a board meeting about what we should do to celebrate Christmas with our workers. We decided to have a barbeque for all the labour force. Great idea! Then, as we reflected, we thought,

But what about the families of the workers? Often Kenyans will travel in to Nairobi from the countryside for work during the week and travel home at the weekend. How will a barbeque help the workers' families?

17 Roy Coad, *Laing: The Biography of Sir John W. Laing, C.B.E. (1879–1978)*, (Hodder & Stoughton: 1979), pp.138, 140, 215, 145.

18 Mark Greene's theology of work, and his definition of work, may be helpful here: 'So work includes any activity that contributes to the provision of human needs – cooking, washing, food shopping, car maintenance – as well as those activities that generate money directly.' cf. Mark Greene, *Thank God it's Monday* (Muddy Pearl: 2019), p.37.

It wouldn't. So we changed our plan and gave each worker a food voucher, so that they had to take it back to their families. I am sure they could find a way to trade it, but food for a family celebration was our intention. The voucher was worth about 3 days' pay, so nothing significant (for us). We gave the vouchers out on Christmas Eve and one worker was heard to be singing (a made up song) about how blessed he was, because today he had received a food voucher and now his family would have such a good Christmas. I'm not sure he was a candidate for *Kenya's Got Talent,* but he certainly was very happy.

SO WHAT MAKES A BUSINESS SUCCESSFUL?

In my view, those workers that actually create the value that a business delivers are often not recognized. Everyone in a company has a role to play in creating the wealth that company makes. I don't dispute that some contribute more than others. What I can't cope with is how one person can be worth several hundred times more than another, as measured by their pay cheque.

Sitting in an airport once, waiting for a plane (in case you hadn't guessed!), I found myself sitting outside the VIP lounge. With nothing else going on in my mind, I started wondering who were these 'VIPs'? In this airport, it was those people who could afford, and had decided to spend, the money for a first class ticket. It wasn't that they were 'important'. This led me on to thinking about who really *are* the important people in an airport? I came to the conclusion that it is the check-in staff, the baggage handlers, the customs officers and the toilet cleaners. Without any of them, the whole system would break down – it would be chaos. I believe that business has a responsibility to recognize those that create the value. It is not that everyone should be paid the same, but there needs to be a fair distribution. And fair recognition.

So to come back to the original question: how do we measure a successful business? There are in fact several possible criteria:

1. Producing a desirable product.
2. Producing an essential product.
3. Producing a quality product.
4. Providing an essential service.
5. Providing a quality service.
6. Creating employment.
7. Creating well-rewarded employment.
8. Having positive social benefit.
9. Making a profit.
10. Protecting the environment.
11. Maintaining a competitive price.

I have thought of 11 here; you will think of more. Clearly one or two – for example, profit – are essential. No business can survive long-term without profit. It would be interesting for those of you running a business, or employed by one, to go through the above list and see how many boxes your company ticks.

The next question I think you should ask is:
How many boxes could you tick?
And then:
How many of the boxes would you want to?
I think once you do that, it tells you what sort of business person you are or what sort of business you work for.

At Hand in Hand we have set our aims: one of these was to give money to charity. One day a board member said,

Your desire to give money to charity is laudable but it's an easy thing to say at the moment because we are not yet making any profits. We need to state now how much we want to give away in the future, because when we eventually have 'big' money that decision will become a lot harder.

He went on to say,

I don't care what the amount is, just set it now, make it known and stick to it.

So we did, and our profits strategy is the 40:40:20 rule:

- 40% of our margin goes into charity or social enterprise.
- 40% is reinvested in the country where we make the profit.
- 20% is for the growth of the company and shareholders.

Let me tell you, it is very easy to come up with this kind of promise when there is no money in the company; effectively committing 80% of your margin away is easy when there are no cheques to write. This strategy is public, is on our website and I have just written it here. I regularly mention it when I do presentations. We have made it known so that when, eventually, we are making large returns, it will be very difficult to go back on. In addition, we have started other companies and some of those have adopted this same strategy. For me, this public accountability has been a very important measure, and if we did not fulfil it I think we could rightly be accused of fraud.

Our other aims are:

- Structure in target-related pay, so that hardworking employees earn more.
- Provide apprenticeships on every construction project.
- Pay particular attention to site safety for the protection of our employees.
- Provide quality student accommodation (something which is currently not available in Nairobi).
- Partner with Christian ministries to give them a fair deal in the development of their land.
- Invest in low cost housing for the 60% of Kenyans who live on less than $2 per day.

Basically, we aim to give a fair deal to all parties. We will make money, otherwise we won't achieve any of the above, but – learning from Boots, Guinness and Laing – I believe we can make a social difference and still make money.

And why is making money so important? Because when any endeavour has a social impact which is financially sustainable, you will do so much more than if you are constantly dependent on the generosity of donors. Let me be clear: donors' generosity can achieve so much – and our charity is supported by many generous donors – and the reason the business commits money to the charity is that there are some things that only charity can do. But business needs to wake up to what a difference business can make, and business needs to define what 'good' business really is.

Our aims have evolved over the years as we have been presented with new opportunities, and they should continue to evolve. I hope that, as a board, we will never lose sight of why God has equipped us to do 'good' business, and the difference it can make to those we employ and, potentially, to our competitors.

~~~~~~~~~~~~~~~~~~~~~~~~~~~

One day, I was talking with Lenny. Lenny was brought up in a safe and loving environment, but poor. Living 'on the wrong side of the tracks'. As a young boy, he wanted to live on the other side of the tracks, where the rich people lived. To achieve this aim, he worked 15 hours a day, spent half his life travelling, took risks and eventually became very rich. He succeeded. (I am not suggesting he didn't tick any of the other boxes.) But now he reflects on how he had little time with his wife – who thankfully stuck it through with him and is still there today – and he has no real relationship with his children; he has all the money he could ever dream of spending, but now he has lost the point to life. Is that not rather an empty legacy?

Perhaps Bill Gates felt the emptiness of a life spent doing nothing but making money, and perhaps it was this that motivated him and his wife to give that money away. I have no idea if that's true, but it's worth a thought.

The obvious questions all this leaves are: what do we want to achieve? What legacy do we want to leave? What constitutes 'good' business for you?

WHAT IS A GOOD BUSINESS?

Now it's time to turn to my faith to try and understand the principles of business. I think there is a common misconception that work is a consequence of Adam eating the wrong apple at the wrong time from the wrong tree. It's not: work was given to Adam before the whole serpent-tempting-woman-tempting-man-eating-fruit story. In Genesis 2, the orchard was given to Adam and he was told to maintain it.[19] Right at the beginning, God knew what was best for mankind. To laze around in the sunshine all day eating fruit? No – God gave Adam a job to do.

At the end of a good day's work, I feel satisfied. I appreciate my days off and my holidays because they're a break from hard work. But if I was constantly on holiday, I don't believe I would be satisfied. God gives us satisfaction through work, and this is how God intended it to be. Ecclesiastes explains that the satisfaction of man is a consequence of his effort, and that amassing wealth is the domain of the sinner, because wealth for the sake of wealth is meaningless.[20] Fundamentally, work is good. Good work results in satisfaction for the individual and can improve self-esteem and mental health, although that is part of a larger discussion. But that can be motivation no. 1 for managing a commercial company and creating jobs.

19 Genesis 2:15.
20 Ecclesiastes 2:24–26; Ecclesiastes 5:8–20.

So how do we determine how we conduct business, and how we treat our workers? There is a concept described in Leviticus called Jubilee.[21] Jubilee functioned at various levels, but allow me to explain the quantity surveyor's version of Jubilee:

In the days of Leviticus, each family was allotted a piece of land. Let's say 2 families had 20 acres each, and let's call our 2 families the Smiths and the Browns. Inevitably, some farmers will be better than others – that's just how it goes, I can't explain it, but it is true from my observation of life.

The Browns work their land and the Smiths work their land. The Browns grow wheat: it is dependable, and predictable and provides a steady return. The Smiths hear of a new plant, chilli pepper, which sells for a much higher price than wheat. So the Smiths grow chilli peppers. But what they didn't realize was that they had to invest in fertilizers and nutrients to make chilli peppers grow. When it comes to harvest time, the Browns harvest their wheat, keeping enough for their own needs, and selling the remainder at market which gives them money for other expenses plus a little to spare. The Smiths get a poor harvest and do not have enough to sell to provide for themselves for the rest of the year. So they go next door to the Browns and say,

We're in trouble: we can't afford to live. Can we sell you 2 acres, which would get us out of our immediate problem?
The Browns agree; now the Browns have 22 acres and the Smiths have 18 acres.

Year 2: the Smiths stick to their idea that chilli peppers are a good crop and so continue to grow chilli peppers,

21 Leviticus 25:8–55.

whilst the Browns continue to grow wheat. At the end of the 2nd year, the Browns harvest 22 acres and make a little more money than last year. Unfortunately for the Smiths, their crop is attacked by a pest called red beetle. They try various methods to kill the red beetle – hitting it on the head, setting traps late at night, basically anything to try and kill the red beetle (sorry to you readers who don't like killing animals) – but this red beetle is very resistant. Eventually, they find a spray that kills it, but by the time it's discovered, all the chilli peppers have been destroyed.

Once again, the Smiths have no harvest and once again they do not have enough money to survive the following year. Once again, they go to the Browns and say,

We have a problem, which hopefully is temporary, but would you like to buy another 2 acres of our land to see us through the year?

The Browns say,

Actually we can see your problem and we really want to help. Why don't we buy 4 acres of your land, which will give you some cash in the bank after you have invested in next year's crop?

The Smiths agree. The Browns now have 26 acres and the Smiths have 14 acres. The Smiths, still confident in chilli peppers, plant again. They now know what nutrients to spray the plants with, they know how to kill red beetle and the market price of chilli peppers remains higher than wheat.

Another year commences, at the end of the year the Browns harvest their 26 acres and make a higher return than the previous 2 years. The Smiths have 14 acres of a very lucrative crop. Unfortunately, on the day they go to market, some research is published showing that chilli peppers cause bad breath and that people with bad breath die younger than people with nice-smelling breath. Suddenly, nobody wants to buy chilli peppers. For the 3rd year running, the Smiths have made no money and so make their annual visit to the Browns to request assistance. The Browns are quite flush with cash by this point. They buy a further 4 acres from the Smiths.

I think you can see where this is going. As the Smiths continue to fail in their ability to make money, they are now in a position where they only have 10 acres with which to produce a crop, whereas the Browns have 30 acres. The Browns are getting richer and the Smiths are getting poorer. Should this continue, it would result in the Smiths being very poor and the Browns being very rich.

To prevent this from happening, God laid down an economic system called Jubilee. Jubilee consisted of rules for rest and restoration. A day of rest every week, and a year of rest every 7 years when the land was allowed to lie fallow. And above all, a Jubilee year (a year of grace) every 50 years. In the 50th year, the Browns must give back all the land to the Smiths that they had purchased over the years, and both families must start afresh. The Smiths, learning from their experience of chilli peppers, can grow wheat. You may think that this isn't fair to the Browns who had worked hard and spent money to buy the land from the Smiths. But they hadn't bought the freehold; they had only leased the land for the number of years to Jubilee. So after year 1, when they bought 2 acres, they were actually buying 49 harvests for 2 acres. On year 2 when they bought 4 acres, they were actually buying 48 harvests for 4 acres. So the deal was fair.

There were 2 purposes to Jubilee. Not only was it a safeguard to prevent the Smiths, who had poorer business skills, from becoming excessively financially poor, it also stopped the Browns, who were sharper in business, from getting excessively financially rich, which is equally important.

Why is that good? Because, I believe, wealth holds an allure that distracts us both from God and community. Jesus is not against wealth nor saying that it is impossible for the rich to be saved; thinking that is in conflict with the concept that we are saved by grace. When he said that it is harder for a rich man to enter the kingdom of heaven than a camel to go through the eye of a needle,[22] I believe he is warning about the temptation money brings and how this temptation distracts us from God and our dependence on him. Money makes us appear self-sufficient, and also creates a hierarchy: an upper and lower class mentality which is destructive to living in community with our neighbour.

Now where does that leave our philosophy of business? When God instigated Jubilee, wealth effectively meant the amount of land you had. Today, in the construction industry, wealth is generated through the paying of wages. If I, as the successful business man, pay my labourers so little that they can't afford to live properly, the concept of Jubilee would eventually mean that I would have to give

22 Matthew 19:24.

from my wealth (which I have made by paying such low wages) to the very person I have made poor.

So let us attempt to apply Jubilee principles to today's construction industry in Kenya: instead of paying my labour as little as I can get away with (even if I am doing so in order to give generously to charities that support poor families in Kenya), I should pay my workers according to what the business can afford, so that the Jubilee is implemented *now*. My workers can pay school fees, and live in decent houses and afford medical bills, not because they are dependent on Grant Smith being generous, but because Grant Smith has paid his workers a living wage which is reflective of the value they add to the company.

I am not saying that we should all get paid the same, although some may argue that justification from the Jubilee concept. What I am saying is that there are good margins to be made in construction, and I should pay my workers proportionately for creating value in the business. In addition to being fair to my workers, the other side of the coin is what Jubilee achieved: if I pay my workers more, I will earn less money and that will prevent me from becoming excessively rich and being tempted away from my trust in God. It will prevent me from being allured by what money can buy and losing my focus as a disciple of Jesus Christ. Therefore, a fair payment structure is both for my workers' benefit and mine, although many won't see it like that.

AND NOW FOR FURTHER REFLECTION

To my knowledge, Jubilee was never implemented: I don't believe there is any biblical account of Jubilee being put into effect on a large scale. What does that tell us? Well, perhaps it tells us that the very thing that God wanted to prevent, happened. The allure of wealth consumed the successful families, even though it was in their hands to implement Jubilee. The poor are always at the mercy of the rich. If the rich weren't motivated to make Jubilee happen, the poor could do little about it. How could the poor bring pressure on the rich?

Today it is no different. The poor are generally at the mercy of the rich. How many people are willing to accept less? But this is not some economic ideal, it is a biblical principle: it is the way humanity needs to live together. If we are all created in the image of God, as described in Genesis[23] (which we are), and if we are who we are because that is how God has made us (which we are), then what gives me the right to exploit my neighbour for my financial benefit? How can it be honouring to God, respectful of others made in God's image or, at a basic moral level, acceptable to watch my brother live in a tin shed whilst I enjoy the fruits of the forest (fruits of the forest which are actually tempting me away from a relationship with my Father God anyway)?

This has been my reflection on business, and the aim of HiH business was to create fairly-paid employment so

23 Genesis 1:27.

that, instead of a poorly-paid construction worker coming to a charity and requesting school fees, that construction worker could earn sufficient money to pay his own school fees with dignity and respect. When I ask you to invest in my business, you are effectively sponsoring a child and, at the end of your investment, you get your money back with a financial return. If you give money to my charity, you achieve the same goal (sponsoring a child through education) but you never see your money again – that is what charity is.

In addition to fair pay, we create apprenticeships so that whether their gifting is to sweep floors or to become an architect, we can give an opportunity to children who have moved through our charity projects to get into a career that is fairly paid.

Somebody once asked me what I earn from the business. When I told him, he said I should be being paid double or treble, which was a nice compliment, but did he understand that he was encouraging me into temptation? The difference between our company and most other companies is that we did not start HiHT for my personal income (which is the case for most new companies); we started HiHT for the social outcomes.

That is what we set out to achieve.

POINTS TO PONDER

- What do you want your business to achieve?
- What is the opportunity cost of achieving your aims?
- I wonder if Lenny ever thought about moving the tracks?

CHAPTER 5

YOU NEED HELP

or

HOW TO CHOOSE A PARTNER

I have always been a bit of a loner. My son, Sam, has just got back from holiday with 15 of his friends. I find even the thought of that horrific. Apart from the fact that I doubt I even have 15 friends, the idea of going around in a herd for a week – into restaurants, to the beach – is just a complete nightmare to me and I don't actually think I could cope. In fact, if anything ever happened to Sue, I think I would be quite happy to go on holiday on my own. I live in Chelmsford, the home of Essex County Cricket, and I often go to watch cricket on my own. Some people think I am weird, but it really isn't an issue for me. I get on very well with myself, rarely argue with myself (although I do have interesting debates) and enjoy the same music as myself; I am just downright good company for me. I often think that in my old age there would be a temptation to turn into a hermit, although you have to be rich, really, to do that properly, and live in a large country manor that becomes progressively more overgrown and derelict.

At the age of 28, I set up a quantity surveying consultancy and worked largely on my own for 20 years. I have never had to play company politics – there has been no stepping on the person below me; there was no one there to step on. There has been no chasing promotion; there was nowhere to go. I provided a service and charged a day rate. If I was of value, my clients kept employing me; if I was no good, I didn't get any more work with that company. All the time I was a consultant I only worked for about 5 companies, so I must have been doing something right for them to keep coming back. I never consulted anyone about what I should do, who I should work for, where the office should be, what rate to charge, what car to drive; I just decided and did it.

YOU NEED HELP

I started Hand in Hand in that same frame of mind. I saw a market and went off to supply it – anything from Joint Venture roads to soil decontamination and supplying agricultural machinery. I gave these projects a lot of time and they cost me a fair bit. But none of them worked.

You need help.

Lorilee had been listening patiently to me for a couple of days. I had met her and her husband, Scot, whilst pursuing another business venture of importing crocodile meat from Malawi. (Which also hasn't worked. Yet.) After hearing my story, Lorilee said,

You need help.

This conversation with Lorilee was significant, not because people hadn't said the same thing to me before, but because this time I listened: it began to make sense. I thought about what Lorilee had said, I couldn't get it out of my mind for days, and I had to admit that she was right. I couldn't do this alone – it's not good for man to be alone[24] – I needed people with a different set of skills, with different expertise, with a different perspective. I needed people to challenge me on the rare occasion when I was wrong. I needed people to encourage me when I was tired – if one falls over the other can help him up.[25] I needed other people.

This was not an easy thing for a loner to admit.

Sue (otherwise known as 'the wise one') had always been *on board*, but it was time for her to join The Board: The Business Board. Gordon, who became known as 'pump man', had been in business most of his life; he had moved from being an estimator to CEO and then Chairman. It felt as though I had known Gordon all of my life through church, and although we disagreed on pretty much every subject whilst serving on the leadership team together, I had a huge amount of respect for him and knew the business would benefit from his input. The third invitation went to Mark, otherwise known as 'nail man'. Mark ran his own business, was a smart operator and shared my belief that business had a response to make to poverty. I needed to invite these 3 onto our board formally – a voluntary management board

24 Genesis 2:18.
25 Ecclesiastes 4:10.

– and make myself accountable. And so the Hand in Hand voluntary management board was established.

I realized that for this to work, for me to work well with other people, I would have to respect these members and be prepared to listen to them. And they in turn needed to share the vision of what I was aiming to achieve.

There are many challenges when starting a new business, particularly when one of your main aims has a social dimension. Start-ups involve an idea, an expertise and a concept. But those involved in the start-up won't have all the expertise of running a business. A board of directors can bring a breadth of experience and knowledge that would otherwise be lacking. Ideally a board should include people with the following experience:

- Finance
- Legal
- Business (preferably the business market you are entering)
- Marketing.

The next problem is that you have no money to pay for this knowledge. Apart from the challenge of finance and cash flow, you need to find capable people with the above expertise who share your business vision, but who are prepared not to be paid. In the early years of a business, this is when you would form a voluntary management board, made up of individuals who see participating as part of their ministry.

However: beware. As they are voluntary, you could ignore them, and if you do that, you will have no board. To guard against this, HiH business formed a board of strong characters, all individuals who understood and shared the vision and, in different ways, brought a broader perspective to the running of business. And I made myself accountable to this board.

To my mind, the essentials of a board are that everyone is striving in the same overall direction, that the members bring valuable expertise to the table and that everyone is relaxed and comfortable with expressing their opinion. I have sat on boards where, over the years, a divide has developed: everything becomes a fight, people try to score points and almost every decision is compromised. We have been very fortunate in Hand in Hand Group (HiHG) that we have never reached that point. At board meetings we can all express ourselves forcibly and draw a conclusion, and then go for dinner, because there is mutual respect. And that doesn't mean we all have to think the same or there would be no point in having a board meeting, but the members all have the same fundamental goal, which is, ultimately, empowering people.

Our board meetings were always full of rich discussion, out of which informed decisions were made. Often these decisions would not have been the ones I would have made on my own, but they were stronger because we arrived at them as a consequence of input from the voluntary board.

GROUP INTERNATIONAL HQ

I affectionately refer to our offices as Group International HQ, which gives the impression of a large operation at the epicentre of an organization. In fact, it is Charity and I in 2 small offices, in a converted barn on a farm. That's it.

The relationship between 2 people in an office, when there are only 2 people in the office, is obviously close. I have had 2 PAs in the business: Emma and Charity. They know everything about the business, from where we are going, where we have been, how we got here and what our struggles are. Charity gives 100% to make the cause happen (as did Emma when it was her lucky job to work with me), which means challenging me when I drift, encouraging me with texts, telling me when I have lost the plot, and setting fire to the restaurant (as Emma once did at the company Christmas 'Do').

When we first started HiHG, my home office was the hub and from there we moved to my friend Neil's garage. You might think that a garage is a funny place to have an office, but Neil had offices in his garage, where he very kindly gave us desk space. Neil and I shared an office even though we were both doing totally different things at our desks. Although the number of times we were actually at our desks at the same time was relatively rare, many conversations that we had during that time were significant and memorable. One of HiH's ventures was trading in *Haaga* sweeping machines, and it was Neil that got us into the garden shows in prime positions, Neil who provided storage for the *Haagas*, Neil who provided lorries to get to the shows, Neil who I would get agitated with when something didn't work out as we had planned, and it was Neil who would say,

I knew that would never work.

You can probably guess my response?

Why the **** didn't you say that earlier!?

But Neil's greatest impact in HiHG has not been any of the above, but rather his delivery of wisdom about the future of the business. Some of you may be sceptical about how God guides us today in business; let me just say that I don't understand it either, all I can say is that there have been so many times when Neil has spoken, but what he said clearly came from God.

I am not saying that every decision we have made is something God has led us to: one of our board members once said,

On reflection, some our decisions seem as though we are just rolling the dice!

But what I am saying is there have been times when we seem to have heard from God. This 'hearing from God' is not an exact science in my view, but we have prayed; it is certainly worth praying, and certainly worth trying to listen.

The great ideas that have been birthed throughout our adventures at HiHG have often been Sue's – despite me thinking they are my own! We currently have 4 companies and an umbrella group, and Sue is a director for 2 of these, she manages the accounts, shares her opinions and views and keeps me accountable. Over our 33 years of marriage we haven't started to look alike (fortunately for Sue), but we have become closer and closer in the way we think.

Through continual gentle challenges and encouragement, my life goals have moved from things like commanding the top floor of a large construction company, driving a Jag and having a good pension, to realizing that there is so much more to life; and it was that which led us to start HiHG. I can be nothing but thankful to Sue for this. It is more than Sue trusting me, challenging me and pushing me to believe I could be part of something bigger; it is Sue and I standing together, trusting, challenging and pushing each other to see lives, communities and cultures changed.

It might often be my face that is seen, but the only reason HiHG has got as far as it has is because of Sue and her work behind the scenes. HiHG is here today, doing what we do, because of other people's belief, support and confidence in us. I, in turn, would like to think that we have had an impact on some people's lives and have expressed belief, support and confidence that has contributed to some of what they are doing. Above all, there is friendship. I am saying this because I think we all need others. Many people may look at me and think that I have everything sorted, and I know that I come across as fiercely independent. But the role others have played in my life has been immeasurable.

So as you look at the people you are surrounded by, do not hold back praise when praise is due, encouragement when encouragement is needed, affirmation when affirmation is required, or be afraid to challenge when challenge is needed. But above all, trust your friends; trust that they want the best for you, and that when the hard challenges come, they come to sharpen us up, not to bring us down.

FRIENDS ON THE GROUND

As well as the board, it soon became clear to me that in order to succeed I needed to work with local people – in Kenya, in Africa. How would I find them? How would I choose?

Unequally yoked?
Should they all be Christians? The Bible warns about being unequally yoked,[26] and this can be applied to marriage, to sharing a house as a student or to business. Do I apply it in business?

The businesses I work in are not specifically Christian, but the way I work in those businesses might set me apart. For example, my goal of donating 40% of my business income to HiH charity and of providing a pay structure different from the industry standard in Africa might not be viewed as industry norms. Like any Christian, I am called to follow God and to show his love in how I treat those who work for me, to demonstrate Christ's authority over me in how I handle corruption and to structure how I am paid in a way that is honouring to God. For people who are marginalized, I am called to treat them better because God loves me and God loves them, not purely because I have a good work ethic. That doesn't necessarily mean that I should only partner Christians – even if we share the same faith, it doesn't mean that we will view issues the same way. Nevertheless, having a different set of beliefs can make decision-making harder.

26 2 Corinthians 6:14.

Not every glittering networking opportunity leads to gold
There is an organization in the UK called Transformational
Business Network (TBN), a group of business people who
desire to transform lives through their business. There are
several stories that have come out of TBN, but the one I want
to tell you now is about when I was introduced to a man
called Matt. Matt worked for the British High Commission
in Mozambique. The main goal of the High Commission
is taking care of British business interests, and Matt was
responsible for facilitating trade and investment. He asked
if I would be interested in visiting him in Mozambique
in order to explore business opportunities. I am sure you
know by now the answer to that question. I returned home
in the evening, greeted and kissed Sue and enquired,

Do you know where Mozambique is?

Sue: *Why?*

Me: *I am going there to meet my new friend Matty.*

Arrangements progressed, I booked my flights and
hotel, and everything was set. The day before I left, Matt
rang enquiring as to where I had arranged accommodation?

Holiday Inn, I responded.

Matt: *Well, we have nobody staying with us at the moment,
you would be welcome to stay in our home.*

Now, this could have been very risky: I had only met
the man once and then had a few subsequent emails and
the odd phone call. What if we didn't get on? At least with
the Holiday Inn I would be able to retreat to the peace and
quiet of my own hotel room. But I decided to take the risk,
cancelled the hotel, was met at the airport by Matt and was
whisked back to his house, where I stayed for the next few

days. And it turns out that my concerns were completely misplaced: Matt and Debbie (his wife) were lovely, made me feel very relaxed and, amongst other activities, took me to a lovely restaurant where they bring raw meat to the table to be cooked yourself on a hot stone. (I think the best piece of meat I have ever eaten. I am sure that is an exaggeration, but it was certainly very nice!)

Around this time at HiH, we had been thinking about how there was a huge demand in Mozambique for quality agriculture and earth-moving machinery. In the UK, there were many companies who supplied this market very well, but there were others who – shall I say – did not supply this market very well! It was a space that I felt HiH could enter, where we could source quality refurbished machinery from the UK and sell it at a fair price in Mozambique.

Matt introduced me to many business people, all contacts he had cultivated through his position at the High Commission, which is after all about looking after British business interests, and mainly with a view to me sourcing machinery from the UK. I made many contacts and had several actions to follow up.

The most exciting conversation I recall was being asked if I could source a second hand hovercraft, not quite a tractor or digger but in a similar field. Yes, you know the answer, and for any of you interested, you can get a very good low mileage hovercraft for around $7m. My client never actually went ahead with the deal, which personally I thought was a missed opportunity, but that's business for you!

In the end, I made not one single business deal out of this relationship.

You should meet …

Having said that, networks are important. Most of my connections have come from somebody saying,

You should meet …

One day, Peter told me I should meet Gladys. Gladys is a Kenyan, working for Tearfund. At that time, I presented a multimedia presentation with Viz-A-Viz (the youth ministry group) on behalf of Tearfund. Gladys was a scary lady and I didn't think she would have time to see a youth presenter she didn't know. When I called, Gladys said,

You can come on the 20th at 11am, you have 20 minutes.

The meeting lasted 2 hours, and we became good friends. And if you look at our circle of friends in Kenya, many of them started with an introduction from Gladys or her husband Joshua. Once in conversation, I asked a person that had been introduced to me via Joshua what his first impression of me was. The response?

You were introduced as a friend of Joshua's, that gave you 80% credibility; you only had to make up the other 20%.

Take Timothy. I was in Kenya and Gladys rang. She was staying at Dr Wachira's house and thought it would be a good idea if we met. I don't really associate with 'Drs' generally – I am a businessman and although I am not stupid, I am not in the 'Dr' category. I really couldn't see anything coming from this one. We arranged to meet the following day, on the bridge. I duly waited on the bridge, and a jovial Kenyan dressed in colourful African dress walked up to me and introduced himself. We went to have lunch in a petrol station and chatted about our lives.

Gladys knew us both well enough to know there would be common ground. Dr Timothy Wachira is not a businessman, but there are many things we share and we have become very good friends. We now work together in education, and Timothy has come onto the Kenyan board of HiH charity.

Then there was Alpha Contractors, a company working in Kenya and the surrounding countries. We meet a few times doing what I call the 'boxing ring' dance, not talking about anything specific, just getting to know each other. One day, I come up with a tentative proposal and outline the financial structure of a potential project. After I have gone through the structure, Dennis the CEO says,

But it's not about the money is it? There is a bigger picture here?

Dennis went on to sponsor me on a bike ride I was doing to raise money for HiH charity. He offered a generous sponsorship and then added that he would double it if I finished. Like I wouldn't! It turns out that running alongside the business, Alpha Contractors have a charitable foundation as well.

Another relationship begins.

ONE DAY JOSHUA RANG
or RESPOND, DON'T INITIATE

When working in Kenya I have always operated under the philosophy, drawn partly from experience of the culture and partly from knowing how charity works, that I would respond to what others put to me, and try not to initiate. The reason for not initiating is that if I tell you I have a business plan to export umbrellas, you may think that the business plan sounds interesting, but you are too polite to tell me that actually nobody carries umbrellas in the tropics. (This is an extreme example.) Whereas if you say to me,

We really need quality umbrellas and you just can't get them round here at a fair price,

I know that is a good place to explore a viable business. So, while I wasn't consciously sitting by the phone waiting for someone to call, maybe I should have been. One day I came home and Sue says,

Joshua rang, can you call him.

I had only met Joshua once or twice before, but knew he was hardworking, clever and precise. Why would Joshua call me? Immediately I ring back and Joshua says,

How would you like to get involved in house construction in Kenya?

This question must rank as one of the most significant ever put to me. Over the years I have learnt not to get too excited on a first meeting, but Joshua and I met and we discussed the potential to build houses in Nairobi. He explained that there is a growing middle class in Kenya with more money to spend on housing, and a massive under supply. The outcome was that Joshua and I registered a Kenyan company: Hand in Hand Development Ltd (more info on this in the appendix).

WHEN SOMEONE YOU TRUST SAYS 'I KNOW A MAN WHO ...' LISTEN CAREFULLY
or REPUTATION IS A GOOD INDICATOR

Talking to Joshua one day, he tells me of a man he has met called Callisto. Callisto manufactures white goods: fridges, freezers, washing machines. In fact, I am told he is the largest manufacturer of white goods in Zimbabwe. He also happens to be on the board of World Vision. Joshua has been to stay with him – in some fancy place with fantastic views overlooking a lake. As Joshua is talking, I am thinking,

This Callisto is obviously a successful business man operating in a difficult economy, amongst some very poor people, but also has a concern for the poor otherwise he wouldn't be on the board of World Vision.

So I say to Joshua,

Do you think Callisto would be prepared to meet me?

Joshua says to me,

I would guess yes.

I make contact with Callisto, explain my relationship with Joshua and ask if he would be prepared to meet me. Callisto invites me to Zimbabwe for a weekend to stay with him and his wife Lydia. Callisto's driver collects me from Harare airport and speaks very highly of his boss. The house is just as Joshua said, beautifully cut into the hillside overlooking the lake. I realize I have never previously been in a house which has a swimming pool in the lounge. I am not very good with first impressions, but I soon have a firm impression of Callisto as a clever businessman, a man of integrity, a man who attempts to treat his staff better than many employers, and a man who has a heart for the poor. The following day, we talk through the synergy between business and charity. It is a very good meeting, but we come to no conclusions or decisions.

At the airport, as I sat waiting for my flight, I wondered what would happen next.

DRIVE 50 MILES FOR TEA
or TRUST YOUR INSTINCT

Eighteen months later the phone rings. It was Callisto; he was at Luton, passing through on his way to a seminar in Ireland. He and his wife lead seminars on business. Callisto asked if I fancied meeting for a cup of tea. Seeing as he had flown over 4,000 miles, it seemed rude for me not to make the effort to drive 50. I looked at my busy schedule and agreed I could meet him the next day. I actually could have met him later on that day, but I thought that would have looked like I sat around doing nothing all the time.

We met in a café and after the normal pleasantries, Callisto informed me he was putting together a consortium to form a mining company in Zimbabwe. If I understood correctly, non-Zimbabweans are not permitted to mine in Zimbabwe; therefore, he was forming a company with a mixture of Zimbabweans and outsiders. He was looking to raise, from memory, $200m and was asking if HiH would like to be involved.

Close your eyes and jump

As I reflected on the proposal, there were a few things that ran through my mind, the first being,

What do we know about mining?

But the second being,

This is much bigger than any of our current activity.

My philosophy in life is generally to be straightforward, say what comes into my head and think about it later. One of the problems that HiH have is that people who hear about us or visit our website think we are much bigger than we are. This seemed to be the case with Callisto, so I responded,

Callisto, while we would love to be involved in such an investment and these figures don't scare us, the reality is, and it hurts me to say it, this is far bigger than where we are right now.

Callisto: *On the contrary, your housing development in Nairobi is a $30m project; $200m is a natural next step for a company like HiH.*

I had to admit, I hadn't looked at the project in that way, but I could see his point. So I thought further,

We still have the issue that HiH know nothing about mining.

So with a little further reflection, I asked,

OK, I hear what you are saying, why do you think we would say yes?

Callisto: *Because your preference is to partner with Christians and you have a desire that with any business you are involved in, all who contribute to the business should benefit and consequently distribute reward*

THE ACCIDENTAL SOCIAL ENTREPRENEUR

in a fairer manner than we generally see in business,
particularly in mining. I share these aspirations.
I thought that was a fair enough answer, and said,
Then I suggest you send me the criteria for the business
and an outline of what you expect from Hand in Hand.
We haven't done anything with Callisto yet.

~~~~~~~~~~~~~~~~~~~~~~~~~~~~

Sometimes in life you come across people and you are
happy if you never have to see them again. But sometimes
there are people you meet who make you think,
I like this person and I would like to do something with
them.
Callisto and Lydia came in the second category. I have
no idea if my initial feelings are correct. But there was
something about this couple that just stood out. And why
am I telling this story? Because for me, meeting Callisto
was significant, but to date it has gone nowhere. However,
as I was writing this, I decided to text Callisto and tell him
I was writing about him and his wife Lydia, and he replied,
I am in Luton in May, shall we have tea?
Well, if you are flying more than 4,000 miles, it would be
rude not to ...

BELIEVE IN PEOPLE

When my mum died, I said at the funeral there would be no
party afterwards where people stand around and talk about
what a wonderful lady my mum was. Instead, I asked people

to go to others at the funeral and tell them how wonderful they are now, because it's too late for my mum. Also, I am a Scot and have been brought up not to waste money on superfluous extras, like a wake!

As I have been writing I have been recalling a number of people that have expressed a belief in me as a person and in my ability to make things happen. My friend Richard once said to me,

If you put your mind to it, you can do anything you want.
Richard and I spent a lot of time tendering a JV for road construction. Many days were spent in his office in Dar es Salaam in the heat of the city, then driving back to his place in the evening, with the final reward for the day of a walk on the beach before supper. Generally, there was a warm breeze, the sound of the water and the sandy beach, where we would reflect, dream and strategize. He was worse than me for having big ideas. It was Richard who either had the belief in me as stated above, or a general belief in humankind (I never clarified which), that in actual fact we can do anything we want if we put our minds to it.

I have already mentioned the investor who had committed to backing us to becoming the largest contractor in Kenya; when someone says that to you, you can't really turn around and say,

I can't.
You have just been told,

You can.
So you either set out to prove them wrong, which would not be the most intelligent response, or you get boosted by

those words and get on with it. To have people believe in you is so important. Let me ask you a question:

How many people do you believe in that you have never told?
When you see something good in a person, tell them. You never know, your words may just give them the *umph* to go and do something really special.

When things go wrong
However, things do go wrong in business relationships, and in my experience it takes time for your differences to surface. The typical challenges that face business relationships can look like any of these:

- Holding different expectations of the outcomes.
- Cultural differences, as in my umbrella illustration: people can be too polite to tell you when something is a bad idea. They would rather you put in investment, a lot of work, and come to that conclusion yourself.
- Lack of experience in the field of execution.
- Personality incompatibility.
- Lack of understanding of the local market.

The greatest challenge I have found is that of aligning expectations, goals and outcomes. Many people will claim they have a desire to make a social impact, or an impact for the kingdom of God, but when the rubber hits the road, or things get difficult, that actually can become less of a priority. This difference has happened in partnerships I've been in on several occasions and has been the biggest reason for falling out. Part of the problem is that one party doesn't want to jump to the conclusion that the relationship isn't working, so you keep at it and at it and at it, until eventually you realize you are on a train with someone but you want to be going to Birmingham and they are actually going to Portsmouth.

Dissolving a partnership is generally not at all desirable, almost always painful and at the very least disappointing. It is a hard decision to make. You try many different things to see how you can make it work, until eventually you know you have to bite the bullet and end it before it gets worse.

And there is a big difference between friends and business partnerships. Most of us would probably subscribe to the well-worn advice, 'never go into business with friends or relatives', however, my experience is mixed:

- Sue is a director and it has never resulted in a clash (so far).
- One of our other UK board directors has been a friend for 30 years, in fact we have been family friends, and we have never had a clash (so far).
- In fact, the members of the voluntary management board were all friends, but they were friends with expertise, and people who I knew would stand up to me.
- Although I wasn't a business partner, I worked in various capacities for a building company owned by a friend for over 20 years prior to HiH, and only remember 1 serious bust up.

So it can work, but it's playing with fire. That doesn't mean that business partners can't be friends – they can, but beware: business with friends can sometimes be at the expense of the friendship. It's a risk you take.

Starting well

If you have an idea and are considering a business partner, here are the things I would look for. Let's call the potential partner 'George'. You can score each point out of 5 as a helpful indicator of your assessment of the relationship.

1. Length of time you have known George.
2. Whether you and George share the same faith.
3. Whether you and George have the same goals.
4. Whether you respect George.
5. How much you can trust George.
6. Whether you and George share the same work ethic.
7. Whether George is available to work (i.e. what other commitments does he have)?
8. Whether George's partner shares his appetite for this adventure.

If you score more than 40, you can't add up. You need to decide for yourself what are essential to score 5.

You might wonder at number 7. Let's say George has a young family and is captain of the local golf club, and your business is in Australia. I can see challenges ahead. That doesn't mean the partnership can't work, but it is a consideration that needs to be worked through.

And number 8: again you may not consider it to be essential, but if George's partner enjoys a steady income and is going to worry that the words 'steady' and 'income' will no longer appear in the same sentence should George go into business with you, then that also needs to be worked through.

Next write down and agree what you want to achieve. Possibly 10 points may look something like this:

1. Deliver a quality product.
2. Employ at above minimum wage.
3. Make sure the customers' needs always come above the money.
4. Create 5% employment for people with special needs.
5. Give away 85% of margin to the homeless.
6. Avoid all forms of corruption.
7. Work 60 hours a week.
8. Travel 5 times a year.
9. Keep a balance of £50k as reserves.
10. Never have an overdraft.

Again, why number 5? That should be agreed when you have no money. When your margin is £5m, it is far harder to say,

Shall we give away £4.25m?

One of my board members gave me that piece of wisdom, as you will remember.

And then appoint your voluntary advisory board. It could be just 2 people you respect; make it clear what you expect from them, and then share your goals.

Because I have seen the benefit of an advisory board, I in turn sit on a few boards. And in my humble opinion, most people don't know how to use them – and yes, the word is 'use' them. If you are not willing to listen to your advisory board and not prepared to take the big decisions to your board, don't waste their time or yours. You may also state that you want their commitment for 3 years as a voluntary board, and then they would have the option of becoming board members who benefit financially from their involvement. That's a choice you can make, but don't promise them 50% of the business on day 1. The reason they should be prepared to sit on your voluntary board is to support you to fulfil your vision. If you need to entice them with money or shares, they are the wrong people. Some may disagree with that; and it is also possibly true that if they either invest or receive benefit they will apply themselves more seriously.

POINTS TO PONDER

- Surround yourself with people who know better than you and listen to them.
- Concentrate on what you are good at.
- If you believe someone has some great qualities, tell them.

CHAPTER 6

I'VE GOT AN IDEA

or

THE ONES THAT GOT AWAY

Sue says that she is going to write on my gravestone,

Grant Smith:
I've got an idea.

I want you to understand that although we always try to listen to God, and we have had a lot of good ideas and we have worked very hard to make them work, fundamentally we have also made loads of misjudgements. I think it is important to understand while you read this book – which is a tribute to God working out his purposes and equipping us to experience great miracles – that there is no formula, in my experience, to getting it right first time. Does that mean we don't trust God? Not at all. I write these stories to encourage you not to give up when you feel like you have fallen at the first, second or tenth hurdle.

I seem to spend my life having ideas, and, to be honest, most of them don't work out. So here are some of my ideas that were either at the wrong place, the wrong time, the wrong continent, the wrong product, or possibly just downright wrong!

I'VE GOT AN IDEA
or BUILDING ROADS WITH COMBINE HARVESTERS

Our very first business idea was to build roads in Africa. I still have that first email, dated January 2000. It happened like this: one day I was sitting on a bus in Tanzania travelling from Dar es Salaam to Iringa. There were roadworks, so, stuck in traffic, I gazed out of the window and watched, on one side of the bus, contractors digging up the road, piling the rubble into the backs of lorries and transporting it away. On the other side of the bus, lorries were bringing new stone, putting it in the excavations and tarmacking to create a new road. Pretty standard procedure, and whilst different countries adopt different methods of construction, the mechanics themselves are generally the same. One major difference in the UK, however, is that we tend to set up diversion lanes whilst construction is in progress, but in Tanzania they tend to let you choose your own route!

The Germans were the first (I think) to look at this problem and to begin to consider if there was an alternative way to fix roads more efficiently. They came up with the idea of an adapted combine harvester. Basically, instead of having diggers, a combine harvester, using a huge steel drum embedded with teeth, eats the tarmac then breaks it down inside the machine, squirts black glue on it and out the back comes a new road. All you need is a combine harvester, a glue tank and a road roller. The combine harvester is 2m–3m wide, and in perfect conditions you could lay 1km–2km of road per day. Sounds unbelievable, doesn't it? You can check it out yourself; it's called a Wirtgen WR2500S and in those days it was revolutionary technology, although today they are commonly used in road construction around the world.

Coming back to the traffic jam: I was a quantity surveyor at the time, freelancing for a UK company, let's call them RoadbuildersUK, who specialized in this method of road construction. So my mind started to wander and I asked myself,

Why don't we form a JV with a local contractor and build millions of miles of roads, make bundles of money and put that money into HiH charity?

Seemed pretty simple at the time. All we had to do was find a reliable local partner, persuade RoadbuildersUK that it made sense, and count the money as it started rolling in.

I was actually on my way to meet the Archbishop of Tanzania. Funnily enough, the Bishop wasn't a road contractor, but, believe it or not, his brother, Dennis, was! The first email I sent for the business was to the Bishop's brother in the year 2000, introducing myself and suggesting that we meet to explore my idea.

Dennis was an interesting guy. He lived in Dar es Salaam and was a successful contractor in roads and construction – he had obviously undertaken some sizeable contracts. So, having identified a potential partner, let's call them Roads of Tanzania, I then discussed the concept with RoadbuildersUK, who also cautiously liked the idea. Job done then! All that was left was to buy a big enough calculator that could cope with all the zeros.

Around the same time I was introduced to Terry (more of Terry in Chapter 8) who knew a Kenyan road contracting company – let's call them Kenya Highways, indigenous to East Africa – and organized a meeting.

Our plans progressed slowly as we began to get to know each other and then started to identify potential projects to tender for. Meanwhile, we continued discussion with RoadbuildersUK; however, I think the more they thought about it, the higher the risk seemed to them. Eventually, they concluded that it was just a bridge too far, or, more accurately, a continent too far, and they withdrew. It was obviously a significant blow.

At this time there were only about 5 contractors in the UK working with this technology, so I promptly approached the others. Very quickly, I entered discussions with one of these competitors – let's call them English Country Lanes – and continued to progress the project. To cement the relationship, our African partners, Roads of Tanzania and Kenya Highways, came to the UK to meet English Country Lanes, and then English Country Lanes visited our partners in Africa. Roads of Tanzania had got us onto some tender lists, there was a project we were tendering for and the date for submission of the tender came. The Tanzanians had priced their side, but there was nothing from the UK. I was anxious, but then the English Country Lanes guys sent over their tender, the 2 prices were merged together, and we came to within minutes of submitting the tender. Then English Country Lanes rang me and said they now wanted to withdraw.

This was the second major blow! I received this phone call around 3pm UK time (5pm in Tanzania) so I phoned Dennis and told him to stand down. I don't know what he thought of me at the time (I can only imagine, although I don't think he ever expressed it himself). At around 4.30pm, I received a call from RoadbuildersUK, who asked if I would like to go into their offices to talk about … yep, you guessed it: building roads in Africa! They had had a rethink and would like to revisit the topic.

In the space of 24 hours I had experienced:

1. Frustration that the UK contractor, English Country Lanes, hadn't submitted their price.
2. Excitement that we were actually able to get the price for Roads of Tanzania to Dennis in time to merge the 2 prices for the 5pm deadline.
3. Devastation, that with 2 hours to go, we no longer had a UK partner.
4. Embarrassment as I explained to Dennis we couldn't submit the tender.
5. Confusion as the original contractor, RoadbuildersUK, came back on board.

Now once again working with RoadbuildersUK, we arranged a visit to Kenya and Tanzania to continue exploring the potential, and again, the feedback from both sides was promising. I think at this point in the story, I will put an end to your suspense and tell you it never happened. From memory the swing swung several more times over a period of 4 years, but the story ends there. We never finalized a contract, we never laid a road, we never made a penny – it just didn't happen. To my mind it was a great idea, and very simple to implement. Perhaps tendering for the road from Mombasa to Kampala was a bit ambitious, but somebody had to do it!

So, after 3 years, having jumped every hurdle, dotted every 'i' and crossed every 't', having financed several trips to Tanzania and Kenya, and having spent 3 years building relationships, cajoling and making decisions, basically it all came to nothing. At the time it was devastating, but you either get up and brush yourself down or go and lick your wounds in the corner.

I'VE GOT ANOTHER IDEA
or WHEN YOU SEE A HEAP OF EARTH, IT'S BETTER NOT TO ASK WHY

Driving along in Kenya one day with a friend, I happened to notice soil being deposited over a large area. When I say soil, I am talking 1000's of tonnes of the stuff. I enquire of my friend, what are they doing?

Friend: *It's the by-product from the cement works.*

Me: *What do they do with it?*

Friend: *They just dump it there, they have been doing it for years.*

Me: *Surely it can be used for something?*

Friend: *I think they make so much money out of the cement, that the by-product is just a nuisance to them.*

So I'm thinking, if the cement works buys loads of vacant land and dumps all this soil, I don't believe that they're not interested in doing anything with the soil. So I reckon it must be contaminated. However, with my experience in soil remediation (which amounted to everything I had just learned from the above conversation with my friend), I am confident it can be cleaned. We could, therefore, be sitting on a potential goldmine!

Pondering this thought, I find a bag in the car, stop to fill the bag with soil, place it in my suitcase and bring it back to the UK for testing. On my return to the UK, I contact a couple of laboratories, explain the situation and enquire if they would be able to analyze it and tell me whether it is contaminated.

Laboratory: *What have you got the soil in?*

Me: *A plastic bag.*

Laboratory: *What was in the plastic bag before you put the soil in it?*

Me: *I don't know.*

Laboratory: *Well, if wasn't contaminated before you scooped it, it is now; you have to collect the samples in 'sample jars' which we can supply you with.*

Me: *Really? OK, send me a couple then.*

So the next time I return to Kenya, I take 2 sample jars, fill them with soil, bring them back through the airport, only to be almost arrested for removing minerals, talk our way out of that and deliver the sample jars to the lab, repeating our investigation.

The lab tells me it is a by-product of extracting cement.
I say,
Yes I know that, but what is it contaminated with?
Lab: *Nothing, it's clean.*
One goldmine, immediately dissolved!!

THIS ONE WILL DEFINITELY WORK
or GARDEN TRADE SHOWS ARE USUALLY AT THE WEEKEND

We had recently taken a big step and taken on a full-time employee to help grow the business. Desmond had previously been selling agricultural products; HiH thought that he might be able to make our machinery sales work and grow in other areas.

It was decided that we would look for a product that Desmond could specifically sell for the purpose of generating finance for HiH UK overheads. It was at this point that HiH were introduced to the *Haaga*, a German manufactured manual sweeping machine which nobody else was selling in the UK. Desmond was confident that the sweeper had a market in the UK and that HiH could negotiate an exclusive relationship with *Haaga* to sell in the UK.

So off we went to Germany, met the directors of *Haaga*, and put our proposal on the table. HiH would have exclusive rights to bring the sweeper into the UK and Desmond would then supply it through a dealer network, as well as selling direct. *Haaga* liked our proposal and a Memorandum of Understanding (MoU) was agreed and signed.

In addition to this, Desmond had also had discussions with a plant hire company who were interested in selling us ex-hire stock which had reached the end of its hire life in the UK. The concept was that HiH would buy the stock in bulk, and then we could either sell it on in the UK at a profit, or send the items to Africa where they could be refurbished and sold into the market place. We therefore had a few ideas in place to generate finance.

Desmond had previously sold through trade shows and was keen to sell the *Haaga* in the same way. Neil, in whose garage HiHG shared an office, in addition to his engineering works, also had a company which sold garden furniture and his main selling strategy was to sell through garden shows. Neil came over to the office one day, and we discussed Desmond's desire to sell at shows. Neil made 1 phone call, and within minutes, he had booked us into 11 shows over the summer, in prime locations next to his garden furniture stands, at a significantly discounted rate because we are committing to all 11 shows and because we were associated with Neil.

Obviously feeling rather excited that we had organized 11 shows, in prime locations, I get on the phone to Desmond to share the good news. This is how the conversation went:

Me: *We have organized 11 shows, in prime locations, to sell the* Haaga.

Desmond: *This is terrific! You had better give me the dates so that I can plan around them.*

Me: **Reels off the dates**

Desmond: *They all include Sundays.*

Me: *Yep, they are weekend shows.*

Desmond: *I don't work on Sundays and I don't believe God will bless our work if we work on a Sunday.*

I came off the phone feeling rather dejected. We had now committed to 11 shows throughout the summer, and Desmond doesn't consider that his beliefs permit him to work on Sundays which, incidentally, I do respect.

HiH were now left with the responsibility of selling *Haaga* at these shows. What I mean is, Emma – who was working with HiH part time – and myself – still working part time as a consultant QS – both with no sales experience, no show experience and neither of us knowing one end of a *Haaga* from the other, were left with the challenge of trying to sell this sweeping machine. We both believed it was an excellent piece of kit, but believing and selling are two totally different perspectives.

Our first show was in Ipswich over the Easter weekend. For 8 hours, we talked, we demonstrated, we laughed, we showed off our *Haagas*. Loads of people stopped to look, but nobody was buying. Eventually the day ended on both a high and a low: a lady wanted to buy 2 of our largest machines – 1 for her drive and 1 for round her pool. Clearly a person with more money than sense, but it would mean about £1,000 profit for HiH. By 6pm, the show was closing and our fellow traders were making their stands safe for the night. In a nutshell, we were knackered, having risen early, put our stand out twice and then walked up and down demonstrating the *Haaga* all day – we were done in.

〰〰〰〰〰〰〰〰〰〰〰〰〰

Ultimately, the shows didn't work for us and eventually the board took the big, grown-up decision to stop selling at the shows.

At the same time, we also had the end-of-line stock from our friendly plant hire company, which we decided to sell on eBay. HiH had a storage facility a few miles from our home (given to us for free by a sympathizer), where we stored the items we purchased. Emma would photograph them all for sale online. The hours we spent out at the storage in the freezing cold, photographing old plant hire items and then excitedly watching them sell on eBay, have not been added up. But the question had to be asked: was this really where we should be directing our efforts?

THE DEBRIEF
or TIME TO BE BRUTALLY HONEST

When you are involved in any activity, whether it be a charity or business or church, or whatever, it is important that you analyze your achievements and in so doing be totally honest regarding the input and output. We sat down with the board and a couple of close friends who were good at working these issues through and described:

- what we wanted to do,
- what we were already doing,
- where we were going,
- where we wanted to go.

The conclusion of this investigation was that I kept looking for some superhero to come into HiH, pick up my ideas and then fly with them, when actually I needed to give up UK surveying and commit myself to making HiH work. Obviously, I could see the merit of this, but of course giving up UK surveying meant releasing our financial security, which wasn't a pleasant thought.

We discussed all this at length as a board and eventually set targets for *Haaga* sales. We did get an invitation to pitch the *Haaga* at McDonald's HQ, and had we been successful there, who knows how the story would have turned out. Basically, we still had the challenge that, although it was a good product, the alternative was ultimately a brush which required no maintenance and no spare parts. When you have that sort of competition, it's difficult to convince people that the *Haaga* is a 'must have'.

It will come as no surprise that the targets set by the board were not achieved, and one day at a board meeting, *Haaga* and second-hand tools were discussed at length and it went to a vote. Let's just say there was an overwhelming majority (of which I was not a part) concluding that we would stop the *Haaga*. Mark, one of our board members, agreed to buy all the current stock on the understanding that he would take Emma and I to dinner in some swanky London restaurant when he sold them all. Well, dinner in London never happened, so you can draw your own conclusion from that.

And the point of the story?

Taking the decision to stop selling *Haaga* was not mine; it was the board's. It was the right decision, but if it had

I've got an idea

been left to me, we could still be selling them. *Haaga* didn't make a loss, but neither was it worth the effort that we put into it. And that is why every entrepreneur should have a board to which they are accountable. Because what was painfully obvious to the board, and to you the reader, was not obvious to me at the time. So we argued and discussed as a board, we had a difference of opinion and the board won. Why is that good? Because the board were correct. That is why you need a board. A board you respect, a board who can say it how it is, a board who share your objectives, but who steer you with their expertise and experience and consequently stronger decisions are made.

And Desmond?

Well, clearly that decision didn't work for us. But again, it could have done. It highlights that there is no fail-safe formula when it comes to business. So Desmond was well-intentioned, had clear capabilities, but we saw things differently.

There were other failures which I won't detail here. But this is an important chapter. Without it, you might think that one day, God told us to start HiH the business, we walked into Kenya, planted a farm and built some houses. But there were both mistakes and poor decisions made along the way and I would say that it took 10 years of poor results to get to where we are now. How many people give up after year 9? I either had an inner conviction that this was going to work, or it could be that I got to the point of no return and just had to keep going. I sometimes deliberate over making a phone call, because I know what I want to say, but am not sure how to say it. I sit with the phone in my hand and look at it like it is going to give me the answer, and then I decide to just dial the number; once the person picks up, the words will come – and they always do, because in a sense they have to!

Yet again, I believe that a significant reason we got through those 10 years was because of the confidence and belief expressed in me by friends. More significantly, possibly, was a conviction felt by all of us that God was with us, and there was something we were called to do to alleviate poverty through business – we just couldn't work out what it was. In business, you are making decisions all the time; the trouble is that, when you make them you don't know if they will work. But if you make no decisions, nothing will happen; if you make a decision, something will definitely happen. It could be good, or it could be disastrous. That's business.

POINTS TO PONDER

- If business was easy, everyone would do it.
- If at first you don't succeed, have another go.
- Keep your overhead costs as low as you can when you are starting a business.
- If your board stops believing in you, go and get a job!

CHAPTER 7

HOW TO CHOOSE YOUR PEOPLE

or

INTERVIEWS AND PERFORMANCE-BASED PAY

Employing someone is a big step. I remember the night, in the very early days, when the trustees of HiH charity felt that we had reached a ceiling; that we would never increase our income whilst we remained a bunch of volunteers. If we wanted to continue the growth we'd been achieving, we had to employ someone. I remember that night was not a comfortable night's sleep. I knew the challenge was right. Up to that point we simply raised money and gave it away. We never committed anything to anyone; if we didn't have the money, we didn't give it.

The minute you take on an employee, you have to find a salary – every month, month after month; you have to cover rent and photocopier ink and Internet and travel expenses. And suddenly there is a pressure. On top of which, if the employed person didn't increase the income, we would be consuming everything we raised. But we knew that this was what had to happen.

At this time, Pete was applying for a job at Tearfund. How ironic! Here was one of our trustees applying to Tearfund, the organization I had said was better than anything new that could be started; surely, we should employ Pete! That, then, was sorted; but what about the cost? We decided to go to our friends, those who were already supporting HiH, and tell them we were going to employ Pete and ask them to sponsor the costs just for 1 year. These friends agreed, and so employing Pete was not a drain on the money we were giving away. Although our model has evolved since that time, in HiH charity we have continued to work this way; our overheads are either sponsored, or are paid through the reclaim on gift aid or direct gifts for overheads, so that every penny raised from our general supporters does go to our projects.

EVEN WHEN IT'S A PERFECT FIT ...

Some time later, someone said to me,
You should meet a friend of mine, Ben Clark.
I have adopted the philosophy in life, that if someone says,
You should meet ...
or
You should talk to ...

I think I should. And I generally always do.

Why?

Because when I studied theology, there were some lectures that made me question why I had bothered getting out of bed in the morning for them! They were so 'nothing' that I couldn't understand why the lecturer, or I, would actually use valuable air space to breathe and waste going through the completely pointless lecture; in fact it led me at times to think that if there is a God, why does he allow me to suffer these things, when I could actually be better off in bed.

And there were other lectures which, in the space of 50 minutes, could change your life.

The trouble is, you never knew at the start of the lecture which would be which. It wasn't that one particular lecturer, or one particular subject, was always life-changing; these life-changing moments could pop up at any time, you just never knew when. Therefore, in fear that I may miss out, I got out of bed and attended every lecture.

That same philosophy has taken me to many places, including Brazil, Uganda, Mozambique, Malawi and Zimbabwe, solely for the reason given above. Sometimes, such trips have resulted in absolutely nothing, and sometimes these trips have changed my life.

So, given that Ben only lived in Southampton, this seemed a small challenge. In the end, it was even better in that I didn't have to go anywhere! Ben and his wife, Helen, came and had dinner with us. (Even for those life-changing lectures I still had to turn up – the lectures never came to me!) Ben had worked for a company local to his hometown and had played a significant role in taking that company from a local to a national level. Ben believed that his understanding of business could be used in Kenya to facilitate Kenyan companies to grow. Consequently, he and Helen were considering relocating to Kenya.

Whenever I meet people like this, I like them. In life there are 3 categories of people according to the Grant Smith structure:

1. Self-consumed
   These are people who are so consumed with themselves and their daily lives that they never look outside their little box to consider anybody else, to do anything to help anyone else or to consider that they owe anybody else anything. Frankly, they are aware that the world goes round, but have a mentality of: *Don't interfere with me, I have enough problems of my own.*

2. Talkers
   These are people who are aware that we are members of the bigger society, that we do have a responsibility to do something to play our part as world members and believe they do have something to offer. They get to the point of talking about what they would either like to do, or could do, but never actually get off their bottom to make a difference, and as the coffin lid is screwed down, you can still hear them!

3. Just do it
   These are, in my opinion, rare. They see the need, they are prepared to do something about it even if it is a cost to themselves, they believe they can have an impact, but they rarely talk about it: they just do it.

Ben and Helen are 'just do it' people, and when you find them, you can do nothing but respect them.

We talked about Ben and Helen's life up to that point and some of their adventures. It was clear they were two very capable people and were 'together' (as the Kenyans say) in their desire to go and work in Kenya. I therefore suggested that Ben might like to come with me and see what HiH do, and perhaps meet some of the people we work with. This we arranged, and duly we flew to Kenya, staying in my friend Joshua's apartment.

One evening, I introduced Ben to Peter. Peter works in oil: importing and exporting. As the evening went on, Ben and Peter got into heavy conversation related to the oil industry. I slowly realized that my only contribution to the discussion was to keep them well supplied with tea as my understanding of their conversation was rapidly diminishing! What this showed me was that Ben's understanding of business went well beyond his understanding of the business he had helped to develop; he actually understood the underlying mechanics of business – he understood business itself.

Ben met a few people, digested the information and then decided he had enough – enough information and enough of me, and flew home early so he could play football on Saturday morning. A man dedicated to the cause! Perhaps that sounds sarcastic, but actually, I don't think we are that dissimilar – Ben had decided he had done what he had come to do, and therefore there was no point in hanging around any further; it was time to go and play football. And although I don't share his love for football, nor, I am sure, his ability, I would have done the same.

Over the next few weeks, Ben and Helen obviously came to the conclusion that their initial thoughts were sound, and they planned to sell up in the UK and move to Nairobi. Ben was still strong in the belief that his understanding of business could facilitate Kenyan business growth, which in turn would create employment, and Helen was potentially able to use her nursing background. The original intention was for Ben to operate as a consultant. If my memory serves me correctly, as a new entrant to Kenya, the main way for Ben to be able to get a work permit was to be employed already. This was obviously a bit of a setback, as he didn't have an employer.

As we chewed over that dilemma, we started to explore the angle of Ben actually being fully employed by HiHT; in this capacity, Ben could do some work with us developing our business, and we could consult Ben out to other organizations for him to do what he does best. This slowly crystallized, and eventually Ben and Helen moved out to Nairobi and found an apartment, funnily enough 50m away from Joshua's.

At that time, we were planting a jatropha farm (jatropha is a source of plant-based bio-diesel and you will learn much more about it later). Ben was working as a project manager for the farm, alongside our Kenyan workers, to plant 70 acres. In addition to that, Ben had some other consultancy work which he tried to develop himself. When I was in Kenya, we would meet up and go through the options for consultancy that were on the table. Ben would also come out to our construction business and introduced me to some contacts that he made. Helen was splitting her time between nursing and charity work.

Sometimes I would stay with Ben and Helen, and sometimes elsewhere – like 50m up the road with Joshua! Ben tells the story of how, before he and Helen were married, Helen was working with a charity in northern Uganda and during that time there was always fighting in the area. This was serious, to the extent that whenever Helen went out of the compound they were stationed in, she had to be accompanied by armed guards.

My mum used to warn me about traveling to Uganda because the official information on the tourist website was that you should only travel if you were on essential business. What my mum didn't appreciate was that I rarely moved out of Kampala, and the greatest threat to my safety was being run over by a motorbike.

Now Helen, on the other hand, was in proper life-threatening situations. Ben continues his tales by describing one evening when they were chatting via MSN Messenger (this was in the days before Skype), an attack was taking place nearby and everyone was advised to get on the floor. So there was Ben on Messenger with Helen, who tells him that there's shouting and – to make it even more dramatic – bullets, and then suddenly nothing; no more responses from Helen because she's taken refuge on the floor in darkness and has had to turn the computer screen off. For those next minutes, Ben was probably engulfed in complete terror, as he had no idea what was happening; wondering whether Helen is OK; wondering if the compound has been overrun by terrorists; wondering what is going on. Then, after everything dies down, Helen comes back online and Ben learns all is well. A truly scary experience.

So it did make me smile somewhat, when Helen was adamant that Ben shouldn't ride a motorbike in Nairobi, because …

… it was too dangerous!

Too dangerous? What, more dangerous than living in a war zone, travelling everywhere with armed guards, and bullets whistling round your ears whilst having a romantic chat on Messenger with your future husband? Admittedly, the rules of the roads in Nairobi are 'survival of the fittest' – or to put it another way: 'survival of the most ignorant' – when there are *matatus* (public minibuses) driving down the pavements behind unsuspecting pedestrians and head on into oncoming traffic on roads that are far too congested; but as dangerous as a war zone?

I don't think so.

All of that is an aside to what took place over the next 3 or 4 years, which I think could be best summed up as:

Slow.

The number of leads that Ben pursued, the number of positive conversations, the number of potential opportunities, the number of raised hopes, the number of recommendations, was huge. But after years of such conversations and not very much work being completed, eventually we were forced to reach the conclusion that we couldn't do it anymore.

And indeed, that was the eventual conclusion that Ben had to accept. Not because his insight to business was non-transferrable to another culture, not because business is run any differently in Kenya, not because Ben's skills were applicable only to one industry and the demand for input was in different disciplines, but simply, in my opinion, because it just takes so long to establish relationships, trust and understanding in what Ben was capable of. Which is a real shame and obviously leaves you questioning all sorts of things:

- Have I got nothing to offer?
- Am I too expensive for the local market?
- Why did I bother giving up a comfortable life?
- Was this all a big mistake?

And these are just my questions; I am sure Ben and Helen have many more.

So, if I met another Ben, what would my response be? If I met another person who had a real zeal to impact people's lives, who believed they had a skill set that could benefit others on a big scale, how would I respond? Well, I think my response would be exactly the same. Because I believed in and admired Ben, because I respected a 'doer' and always will, and I hope that this experience has neither dampened Ben's spirits or anybody elses' who might be thinking of giving up their comfort zones to make an impact somewhere else.

Why am I telling this story? Because, too often, people write books or preach from pulpits and only tell the successful stories. Or, more to the point, the stories that appear successful to our human eyes. But the truth is, even when you are focused, targeted and driven, there are numerous brick walls that you have to break through; nothing is plain sailing, and every wall you come to, you have to grit your teeth and fight your way over it. But it's more than that, because you also have to be discerning enough to decide when to pull the plug – and pulling the plug is usually a harder decision to make than to keep on going, strange as that may sound.

Why do I say that?

Because if you are gutsy enough to stick your head above the parapet, you are not the sort of person who is going to easily accept that it's time to stop.

Often we simply don't know what God is doing through us and we can be really frustrated and disappointed when things don't turn out how we expect. But success in God's eyes is often failure in ours. Learning to trust him, whatever the outcome, is what true faith is all about.

MAYBE JUST DRAW LOTS?

I have written about how I chose a partner, but what about an employee who contributes to decision making? Well, firstly, evidence of knowledge and experience in the role is very important. It is preferable for the person to share our purpose, but not essential. Sharing our ethics is imperative. You see, I can vouch for myself 100%. The minute you employ somebody, you are then trusting them to work by the same ethics to which you subscribe.

I was interviewing candidates for a consultant's role, and one person being interviewed made an unfortunate joke about corruption. I actually don't think he meant what he said, I think it was purely a joke, but it was a very badly timed joke and certainly inappropriate in attempting to make a 'first impression'. That comment gave a big enough warning to the panel making the employment decision not even to consider employing him. However, whether that was the right decision I have no idea.

Here is a sample tick box with a mark out of 5, which I would want the applicant to achieve in the interview:

Applicant:

Capacity for job role	4
Experience in the job role	4
Shares the vision of the company	4
Same ethics as HiH	5
Vision to expand the role	3
Do I think I can trust them?	5

Let's put this to the test with Pete, who we met at the start of the chapter. We didn't have the above scoring system then, but I will mark it as if we were at interview stage.

Applicant: Pete

Capacity for job role	1
Experience in the job role	0
Shares the vision of the company	5
Same ethics as HiH	5
Vision to expand the role	3
Do I think I can trust them?	5

Pete pioneered the employed work space in the charity, grew our visibility and income, and moved the charity on from a group of volunteers. (Pete later left due to personal reasons.)

Now let's apply the same to Desmond who we employed to progress HiHT, commencing with the *Haaga*:

Applicant: Desmond	
Capacity for job role	5
Experience in the job role	4
Shares the vision of the company	5
Same ethics as HiH	5
Vision to expand the role	5
Do I think I can trust them?	5

Desmond was not successful in the role, and subsequently left because we just weren't really compatible. The question of Sunday trading, and *Haaga* shows being on a Sunday, was a detail that brought this to light.

The point is that, at interview stage, it is a lottery for me! Desmond scored far higher than Pete, yet it didn't work out. Pete had no experience in the intended role, yet he performed fantastically. We prayed about both decisions, we felt God helped us in both decisions; one appointment went against logic and was a success, and one went with logic and was a failure. My conclusion is, perhaps you just draw lots?[27]

---

27 This is actually a biblical way of seeking the Lord's will and making a decision. See Numbers 26:55; Proverbs 16:33, 18:18; Jonah 1:7; Acts 1:26.

PIECE WORK AND PERFORMANCE-BASED PAY

When it comes to construction workers, I would always pay on a performance basis wherever possible. This gives a hard-working person the opportunity to make more money and the lazy person essentially just doesn't work for us. It makes the company competitive and it rewards the construction worker. I would always like to think that anyone who joins us at whatever level leaves a better person than how they joined us. What I mean by that, is either they have received training, or a broader experience, or accepted greater responsibility to take into their next job role. We have to live in the reality that the job market is more fluid today than it was 50 years ago. Fifty years ago, you 'went down the pit' because your father 'went down the pit', and your grandfather 'went down the pit' and that was life. These days, people travel further, and change jobs much more frequently and easily than previously. So when I employ anyone, I recognize that we are only a chapter in their working life, hopefully a long one, but the reality is that they will probably move on, and when they do I want them to be better than when they joined.

POINTS TO PONDER

- If someone tells you to meet somebody, always do it. You never know what it may lead to.
- Don't just talk about something, do it.
- Don't ride a bike in Nairobi: it is safer to be shot at!

CHAPTER 8

PUMPS

Just in case you read Chapter 5 2 months ago and have forgotten where you left off, I talked about the merits of choosing the right partners. However, I didn't mention everyone.

Here is one more: let me tell you about my business partner, Terry, who has subsequently become a close friend.

Terry is Kenyan, a strongly committed Christian, and he began his business life at university taking photographs of his fellow students and friends, and selling the photos back to them. He actually studied civil engineering and after many years of service to the government, Terry's entrepreneurial spirit surfaced again and he began to explore various business opportunities. Having considered a few options, he ended up in commodities.

Terry is now a very successful businessman. You can see from my criteria for choosing a business partner that Terry fitted the basic profile.

I was introduced to Terry by another Kenyan friend, Laura. Laura had heard about my road contracting ideas and thought Terry would be a good person to speak to. I contacted Terry and told him about what I was attempting to achieve. Terry's response was that he knew a Kenyan road contracting company indigenous to East Africa and would be happy to organize a meeting.

We arranged to meet in a petrol station. On the chosen day, at the chosen time, I found a small pickup truck sitting in the car park, with Terry inside it. Terry was a man of slight build, pleasant disposition and was quietly spoken. I remember feeling immediately at ease as we drove off to have tea together. We discussed my ideas and he agreed that the concept had legs and that he had the right person for me to explore a potential relationship with. From here we agreed that Terry would arrange a meeting with the MD of the proposed company.

And so a round of meetings commenced, with Terry organizing each one. One day, I was arranging the next meeting when Terry enquired,

When are we going to have a meeting to discuss business opportunities for the pair of us to work on?

This, I thought, was a fair point, although I wasn't sure where we would find a common business interest. I know how to build just about anything, but I knew nothing about commodities. In any JV (Joint Venture), both parties have to bring value to the table and I couldn't see what value we could add to each other. However, that aside, we began to explore opportunities we could work on together.

On this visit to Kenya, Mark, who was on the HiHG voluntary management board at that time, had come with me. Mark managed and owned a very successful business in the UK, importing and selling through the Internet. The three of us sat down in Terry's office and began to put ideas on the table. The areas that I can remember exploring were:

- oil filters
- windscreen wipers
- batteries
- air filters
- tyres
- nails.

I don't remember how we eventually got to petrol pumps. Mark always claims it was his idea, and it may have been; I'm relatively sure it wasn't mine.

The concept was this: in the UK, all independent petrol filling stations were slowly disappearing and petrol was only being sold by either the multinationals or supermarkets. This meant that the small independents were closing down and disposing of their petrol pumps. Could HiH source these pumps in the UK, containerize them, and ship them to Kenya, where we would set up a workshop to refurbish them and sell into the local market? The outcomes would be:

- Providing a quality product
- Creating employment in our workshops
- Making a profit.

I had no idea how many of these pumps were available in the UK, but we agreed that we would explore the idea. Terry was comfortable that he could set up the workshops to refurbish them, and that there would be demand.

I returned to the UK with my new mission. I mentioned it to Daniel, who worked in the charity office at that time, and he found someone who was selling petrol pumps on eBay in Rayleigh. Gordon, who was also on the HiHG Management Board, and was newly retired from a successful business, was prepared to help and the task of finding pump suppliers began.

After a few months, Gordon had found what was available, what sort of prices we should pay, where we could get pumps and the numbers available. Terry was intending to come over to see what we had found, and my feeling was that we should know what we were talking about before he arrived. So Gordon and I set off to meet these various suppliers.

With our research complete, Terry came to the UK. I had arranged a tour of pump dealers in England and off we set to explore together. 2 days later we returned and, sitting in my office, Terry looked at me and said the following:

I expected you to give me a few telephone numbers of potential pump suppliers, I didn't realize how seriously you would take this. You have clearly been and visited all these suppliers before I came and established the relationship, I am very impressed.

Most white people, when they talk about profit in the business/charity sector, would then tell their African partner what they should do with their profit. But you have never made any suggestion of what I should do with my profit. You have made it clear what you are doing with HiH's profit, but you have left me to my own judgement – that's not normal!

And so the pump business began. We worked out how much we thought we could get into a container from advice we had been given, we calculated the cost of purchase, supply and shipping together and then ...

... Terry wrote out a cheque to finance the consignment.

Now, I wasn't expecting that. What I was expecting was that HiH would have to fund it and, once transported, refurbished and sold, we would receive our return. Having said that, I didn't know how we would have funded the shipment, because we had no money; frankly, we just hadn't worked that out yet. So to be paid up front was a somewhat unexpected experience, but most welcome.

This was March 2006 and the cheque from Terry represented the first significant funds from overseas that came into the business.

Gordon started to arrange transport and lorry-loads of pumps began to arrive on the farm where we had our office. We unloaded, stored and packed the container full of pumps, spare panels, hoses, nozzles and other useful bits. Most pumps still had residue petrol inside them, so as you started to move them around, inevitably, it dripped out and, invariably, I ended up stinking of petrol. It was a good job I didn't smoke, for if I had, I think I may have gone up with a bang!

For any of you thinking that I am directing all of this from my executive chair, let me explain: Gordon would locate the pumps, agree prices, place orders, make the payments and arrange logistics to the farm where we had our office, near Witham. I would be at the farm to receive the pumps – often with Gordon – using the farm's forklift to unload and store the pumps. I would then arrange the delivery of the container and liaise with the clearing agents, estimating how many pumps would fit into the container, the overall weight and its value. Following this – again, often with Gordon, or some other willing helpers or just on my own – I would pack the container with the pumps and other accessories. I would then arrange for the clearing information to be couriered to Kenya, so that Terry's clearing agent could locate the container, get it cleared and pay the duties.

Many a happy Saturday was spent up the farm on my own, arranging and rearranging our pumps in order to try and squeeze one more into the container.

One concern I did have was that, having packed the container and shut the doors, I'd invariably go back a couple of days later to add a few more pumps, and the smell of petrol as I opened the doors was somewhat overpowering; it did make me wonder whether, sooner or later, I would be watching the news, and there would be a report of a shipping tanker having sunk in the middle of the ocean due to an unexplained explosion from within its cargo.

The business grew; we developed receiving partners in Ghana and Tanzania in addition to Kenya (the Ghanaian and Tanzanian relationships were structured in the same way as they were in Kenya).

There are many stories I could tell you regarding the pump business. For your information, you can pack approximately 45 pumps in a 40' container as long as you tightly secure the hoses and remove the side panels, placing the side panels over the top once the pump is packed. I think a pump weighs about

200kg, although I never really knew the exact weight, but they were certainly difficult to manhandle. Although the forklift did the majority of the work, a little manual manipulation was always needed for the last bit. When I came home from packing a container, I was usually exhausted from levering, cantilevering and shoehorning the pumps into the tightest of spaces.

As I said, the arrangement between our partners was 'cost-plus'.[28] This is obviously open to abuse and not normal practice for a new business to be established, and particularly a UK/African relationship. But the principle worked, and it was never abused. There was one occasion I recall, when Gordon had scheduled out a consignment, tabulated the number of pumps, the models, the prices and the transport costs and emailed the table to me. As I opened the mail, I noticed he had accidently copied Terry, therefore revealing our costs. It was at that point I realized that, had HiH been adding a little bit of side profit on, I would have been exposed. However, we weren't adding anything on and there was nothing to expose.

Let me explain the business model:

1. Gordon locates and orders the pumps.
2. Gordon places an order for pumps to be delivered to Witham.
3. Pumps are delivered to Witham, and Gordon and Grant unload the pumps.

---

28 Cost-plus pricing (or markup pricing) is when a company adds a percentage on top of the cost of a product to work out the selling price for the customer.

4. Grant organizes a container and arranges shipping.
5. Grant completes bill of lading[29] for shipping and clearing.
6. Grant loads the pumps and spares into the container.
7. Grant sends the documentation to Terry by DHL.
8. Terry arranges with a clearing agent to receive the pumps in Mombasa.
9. Terry transports the pumps to his workshop.
10. Terry takes responsibility to refurbish the pumps.
11. Terry employs a marketing person to sell the pumps.
12. Terry determines the market price.

Approximate costings for HiH UK:

- Purchase of pumps   £200 each
- Delivery of pumps to Witham   £20 each
- Shipping 20' container   £2,500

Terry's costs in Kenya:[30]

- Clearing and paying duty on pumps.
- Transporting pumps to his workshop.
- Refurbishing and respraying pumps.
- Marketing.

Basically, Terry determined the sale price, we subtracted all our costs and the difference was the margin which was split 50:50 between Terry and HiH.

The business employed a few people; we had 3 workshops, in Tanzania, Ghana and Kenya. In Kenya we employed

---

29 Detailed list of a ship's cargo in the form of a receipt.

30 I can't tell you Terry's actual costs in Kenya, because that would reveal a business confidence.

George full time in sales. George was paid a basic salary with a commission. As you can imagine, you tend to sell pumps one at a time. Occasionally, a person opening a new filling station will want 2, or 4, but generally pumps sales were hard work. One day, we located 18 commercial pumps; we weren't sure if they would sell, but we obtained them at a very good price, so decided it was worth the risk. We were so wrong about the risk! Almost the day they landed, George sold the lot. That month, George was probably the best paid salesman in town. What an achievement!

Another time, however, it was a rather different story. I was in Kenya meeting with George. From memory it was February (and you'll see why that is significant in a moment). George and I were catching up, when George informs me,

You know I haven't had any pumps in stock to sell since October.

I asked George to clarify what he meant.

George said,

I sold the last pump I had in October and haven't had any delivered since.

It was then that I realized that neither Terry or myself had been communicating efficiently enough and that neither one of us had been keeping a close enough watch on our stock levels. My relationship with Terry was going well, but this obviously had to be tackled. Tact and diplomacy have never been my strong suit, but I know I can't avoid this discussion.

Terry enters the room,
Everything OK?
Me: *Well not really. George has just told me he has had no pumps since October, is this correct?*
Terry: *I'm afraid it is.*
Me: *We went into this business because we felt God led us to it together. I am not sure that God would be that honoured by how we are running it.*

Allow me to explain what I mean by 'God's business'. Neither Terry nor I needed this business for our income. Terry is managing a very successful business, and when he got involved with the pumps at HiH it was not to enhance or supplement his income. Happily, I could also earn my income through surveying. The reason we began the pump business was because we believed that God had asked us to do it and the benefits of the business, profit and employment were meeting our desire to serve God. That is not to say there aren't other definitions of doing 'God's business', I am simply explaining our logic.

I had made my statement and an awkward silence followed, broken only when Terry says,
When we go home for dinner tonight, can you say all that again in front of Sarah, my wife.
Why? I enquired.
Terry replied,
Because it's like a good sermon: when you hear it, you know you have to do something about it, but very quickly you forget and nothing changes. But if you say it in front of Sarah, she will constantly remind me to do something about it.

The following day, we were in Terry's office, having tea. Terry had an announcement to make. Before we get to 'the announcement', I need to explain that Terry and HiH had been talking about growing a plant called jatropha. I mentioned our jatropha farm earlier on: jatropha is a bit like castor oil or rape seed oil, but the difference about jatropha is that it grows in semi-arid soils.

Terry said,

I have been thinking through the jatropha project and would like to propose that we go into business together with a view to growing 2,000 acres.

I just stared at Terry with a flood of thoughts rushing through my head, with the main one being,

Are you serious?

As I digested the information, what I actually said was,

Terry, 2,000 acres is a serious business. Given the scale of the pump business, which is nothing compared to this proposal, this is a huge commitment for both us.

Terry looked at me, and with a wry smile, says,

What's the problem, 2,000 acres too big for you?

And that, as they say, was that. I am never going to back down from that sort of challenge; so that day, Hand in Hand East Africa Ltd was formed, a Kenyan registered company focused on growing jatropha in Kenya, with a longer term view that, if we made it work in Kenya, we would roll it out in other East African countries. Alongside HiHEA we formed Hand in Hand NRG Ltd, a UK registered company, set up to attract investment to finance HiHEA.

The pump business continued for a while after that, but sales were becoming more of a challenge as the Chinese were producing pumps which, though not comparable quality-wise, were certainly very competitive in price. Added to this, our attention was shifting to jatropha, resulting in us taking the decision to conclude the pump business.

On reflection, the business had certainly been a success on one or two fronts. For HiH, we had been able to contribute to something that had worked, it supplied a need and was profitable. I have always intended to count up one day how many pumps we supplied in total, but it never created large numbers of jobs, which was one of our aims. It had, however, been a stepping stone in our history to where we wanted to go.

I recall once asking Terry if he considered the pump business had been worthwhile, to which he responded,

If we had never entered business together, we would never have developed the relationship of trust that we now have, so if for no other reason than that, the business has been a valuable exercise to move onto bigger and better things.

As I conclude this chapter, I am asking myself the question: why have I gone into so much detail? Possibly you are asking the same question. The reason, I realize, is that Terry is one of my most significant business partners. We have developed complete trust and have become very good friends. Today we are involved in office block development, but it is important to know the steps we took to get there. We didn't just wake up one day and start building offices. We took simple small steps towards each other, arranged meetings, oversaw a small business in pumps that led onto jatropha farming, that eventually led to office development. We took time to get to know each other – I mean years, not hours. We got our hands dirty, literally. Have you ever been in the back of a 40ft container, surrounded by petrol pumps all giving off fumes? We recognized when it was time to stop, which didn't mean the end of business; knowing we could work together, we moved onto bigger business. It didn't fulfil all our aims for working together, but it built a relationship which has moved on to so many other things.

And the moral of the story is: relationships can take a long time to build and you may not achieve your intended outcomes. But, as I always say:

If you do nothing, it's certain that nothing will happen.
If you do something, then you create the possibility for something to happen.

POINTS TO PONDER

- No project is too small for God.
- No project is too big for God.
- Nothing is forever: as the market changes, be ready to move on.
- What does doing God's business mean to you?
- If you want to transport a petrol pump, make sure you empty it of petrol.

CHAPTER 9

THE CASE AGAINST JET ROVER FARM

or

WHY INVESTORS OFTEN DON'T INVEST IN AGRICULTURE

One day I was talking with a Kenyan friend called Beatrice. Beatrice had been looking at a plant called jatropha, and thought it might have potential. Beatrice had been talking to Terry about jatropha. Possibly Beatrice had talked to loads of people about jatropha, I don't know, but this is where the idea began.

Jatropha: many of you will be asking,
What's so good about it?
I asked exactly the same myself at the time.

THE PERFECT INVESTMENT PLAN

Jatropha is a plant that is widely grown in India and produces oil, much like castor oil. The oil can be processed into biodiesel, but in the unprocessed form it can be a substitute for kerosene. Kerosene has many uses, including fueling aeroplane engines and for lamps. People in rural areas in Kenya use kerosene for cooking and lighting. Jatropha oil can be up to 3 times more viscous than kerosene, which means that a litre of jatropha oil will burn for 3 times longer than kerosene. Because it is more viscous, it is less combustible than kerosene. Often the cause of accidental fire in slums is kerosene being spilt and instantly combusting. Jatropha oil won't do that.

If rural people can't afford kerosene, they use firewood; to get firewood, they need to cut down trees; and cutting down trees for firewood day after day is not sustainable in anyone's language.

Jatropha can grow in semi-arid conditions. It's not disputed that it would also do well in fertile soils – in fact, it would probably do better – but it doesn't do well with large amounts of water. On our farm we had no rain for 18 months; but even though our plants were young, they survived.

There is a good argument against growing oil crops in soil that you could be growing food crops in. I am sympathetic to the food/oil land-use debate, and agree we need to prioritize food over oil, but I also believe we need to find sustainable oil. The ideal solution is to grow oil where you can't grow food, and there you have the perfect answer.

In addition, once the plant is squeezed and the oil extracted, you are left with a residue which is a rich fertilizer and can be sold for additional income. And added to that, the husks can be compressed and made into briquettes.

We decided that, apart from growing jatropha on our own land, we would also want to encourage rural farms to grow it with us, so they too could maximize the use of their land. They had struggled for years being vulnerable to the seasons, never knowing if they would get a good crop or not. HiH would establish a processing plant, turn other growers' seed into oil, and thus create income for vulnerable groups.

The jatropha elevator pitch.

Here's the picture:

> *Jatropha: we plan to grow a crop producing oil, and sell that for cooking and lighting as an alternative to kerosene (which causes fires), and as an alternative to villagers going into the bush to cut down trees, preserving the environment, and creating a by-product of fertilizer. On top of this we will create fair employment opportunities and an environment for training.*

So, Terry, Beatrice and I formed a company called Hand in Hand East Africa Ltd, registered in Kenya. In the UK, we formed an investment company with the sole purpose of raising funds to invest initially in HiHEA, but which, once successful, would invest in other energy projects. We applied to register that investment company as Hand in Hand Energy Ltd, only to find that others had used that name a few weeks prior to our application. Emma then said,

Why don't we apply to register Hand in Hand NRG Ltd?

Spelt differently, but sounds the same. HiH NRG Ltd was registered in the UK and divided into shares to raise investment.

The plan was to start with 70 acres, as this would allow us to experiment. The bigger plan was to purchase and grow 2,000 acres, establish our own processing plant, process jatropha oil and encourage local farmers to grow a similar acreage, where we would then offer them the facility to process their seed.

The end game with the 2,000 acres was that we would employ about 300 people. If, on average, they each had 5 dependants, this would benefit a village of 1,500 people. They would have proper homes (not the normal agricultural houses) with a school, clinic, church and recreation space, creating a structure of reward where our employees benefit from the success of the farm. Our aim, therefore, was to create fair-paid employment, training opportunities and the possibility for advancement, so that agricultural workers could progress to become foremen and managers.

We did not want to encourage local farmers to grow jatropha at the initial stage, as we didn't want to raise farmers' hopes of a viable crop which, for whatever reason, didn't work. We'd have to go back to our rural neighbours who would have cleared their land of other crops that may not have been doing so well, but were at least producing a form of income, and say,

Sorry chaps, got it wrong, the crop won't work in these soils.

We decided to manage the first 70 acres ourselves, with a view to producing the jatropha oil. We considered there was sufficient demand in the rural areas for kerosene which the jatropha oil could supply. However, if this assumption proved to be wrong, Terry, our partner, had a network of outlets which we could then tap into for our own distribution.

And so, we were off! The plant didn't really yield for 3 years or so. In order for a bush to grow, jatropha has to be cut back for the first 2 years. That way, instead of just 1 stem, you aim to achieve 30 to 40 stems from each bush. Ideally you don't want it to grow over 1.5m tall, because harvesting is done by hand, and therefore anything over that height makes it a challenge.

We wrote a business plan with the caveat that there would be no return in the form of dividends for the first 5 years. We wanted investors to come in with us for the long haul, rather than something short term, as we knew this certainly wasn't something that would earn a quick buck!

The jatropha investors' pitch

Now you have investors listening who are interested in investing in:

- Africa
- Social benefit
- Environment
- Agriculture
- Sustainable oil
- Education / training
- Welfare.

Then you get to the questions:

- What track record is there of growing jatropha in Kenya? *None.*

- What track record have you got for growing jatropha? *None.*
- What track record have you got in farming? *None.*
- What assurances can you give that the land has clear title?[31] *None.*
- What guarantees or security can you give? *None.*
- How do you know jatropha really is drought resistant? *We don't.*
- Who else do you know growing jatropha? *No one personally.*
- Have you seen any jatropha growing in Kenya? *No.*
- Have you seen any jatropha growing anywhere in the world? *No.*
- If it's dangerous to animals, is it dangerous to humans? *I'll look into that.*
- Can you give me any comfort at all in this investment? *You know where I live!*
- How much investment have you put in yourself? *Let's move swiftly along ...!*
- *So where do I sign ...?*

When you put it like this, I have to confess, it doesn't jump off the shelf as an investment where you are likely to get trampled in the rush to buy shares while they are still available!

---

31 A title without any kind of lien or levy from creditors or other parties, and poses no question as to legal ownership.

One evening, I was invited by a friend, Simon, to speak to two of his friends about jatropha. I really didn't want to do it. I couldn't see the point, as I had talked to these guys about it before and felt I was wasting my time, and theirs. I went to Simon's house, I spoke about what we were trying to do and at the end of the evening, I had 2 investors. They left and I stayed in the kitchen with Simon.

I said,

Simon, I really didn't see the point in coming tonight.

Simon said,

God told me to get you in front of these 2 guys, because they will invest.

We found initial investment to the tune of £100k raised by 3 people who basically took a complete punt, when they knew that the likelihood was they might never see their investment again. But they invested, for whatever reason; I guess there was a strong element that HiH were trusted, but we were trusted for our integrity, not for our ability in agriculture. It's these times that you are humbled, because effectively you know that you are not in control!

PUTTING THE PLAN INTO ACTION

This first investment was sufficient to make our original purchase of land and to plant the 70 acres. We bought some land in Central Province and began digging. Having never planted jatropha before, we were like new kids in a very big playground. Having read up on the Internet, we had concluded that we needed to dig holes 600mm x 600mm x 600mm, and the spacing of said holes seemed open to experimentation.

After 1 month, we had planted 2 acres; something told us we were going to have to speed up the process! During this time, talking to investors, one response had been that jatropha isn't economically viable under 40,000 acres. If we decided to increase our ambition and go for this acreage, it would take us 1,500 years to plant at our current rate of progress.

We had to increase production, so we purchased a mini excavator. We also continued hand excavation and eventually planted the 70 acres.

We also decided to import a tractor from the UK. Given our experience in importing pumps, this was a relatively straightforward exercise, although the batteries and the oil filters were stolen in transit.

We were making progress and were committed. Either that, or we should have been committed, I am not sure which! We got the first acres planted, and then watched as one challenge after another came to stand in the way of making our farm strong.

THE TROUBLE WITH FARMING

That was the start. Now let me explain my fear of farming: I am a QS, so in my experience, you take a brick, you coat it in cement, you take another brick and after a while, invariably you get a house. Every time! Yes, obviously there are challenges, but I know how to respond to these challenges.

With farming, you buy some land, you plant seeds and then … it seems there are endless possibilities for it to fail.

Water: not enough, too much, or the wrong kind

We start with not enough water, which for jatropha is only a problem in the first year. To tackle that problem, we apply for connection to the local municipal water supply. After about 6 months our application is successful, so one would assume we then had water. Once connected, however, there is actually no water in the pipe due to the time of the year. So we think perhaps we could put a borehole in, but we are advised that this isn't necessary; a well will suffice. We get a water engineer out, who informs us of the best place to dig; we dig, we hit rock about 40ft down, we give up. Not to be put off, we have another go elsewhere on the farm; we dig, and at around 40ft, we hit …

Yep, you guessed it: rock.

This time our well-diggers suggest we apply to the council to use explosives. Permission is granted – now I hope our well-diggers know what they are doing, otherwise our farm could end up in another county and we would have to apply for water all over again.

The next time I visit the farm, we are given the bad news: there is water in the well! Curious, but not wishing to show my ignorance, I thought that was why we had dug the well! I keep silent, but eventually my curiosity takes over. So, I enquire,

Why is water in the well bad news?
We can't dig.

Of course: you can't dig if there is water in the well!

By this time the water from the municipality is on.

That's good, I say.

However, as I watch one of the workers fetching water from a large tank to water the seedlings, I become curious again. Why don't we use the municipal water?

Too much chlorine, it kills the seedlings.

Of course, again, my mistake was to apply logic.

Soon we visit the farm to find the rains have come.

That's good, I say.

Yes, except that there is a small part of the farm that isn't draining and has turned a little swampy, and the jatropha has died. Too much, too little, none at all, with chlorine, water in the well – this water thing is a little more complicated than I first realized.

Red beetle and a little wormy thing

The next problem is red beetle.

How big a problem is that? I enquire.

Not so much, you can spray and it will kill it. But you have to weed between the plants first.

Now I am sure that is a good idea, but not sure why it is connected to red beetle. I am then informed that if we don't weed, when we spray, the red beetle will hide in the weeds and pop back when the impact of the spray has worn off.

Then, a little wormy thing (I am sure agriculturists reading this will be very disappointed with my terminology) seems to impregnate its way into the leaves, and when I say 'into the leaves', I mean inside the leaf. It is almost as if it tunnels into the leaf.

You can spray for this? I enquire.
Oh yes.
But let me guess, you have to weed first?
See, already I am an expert.

A lonely locust and a bad case of mildew

Then there was a locust. Believe this story if you choose; this is my interpretation of what I was told:

On a dark, dark night in the midst of the heat, one locust turned up to our farm. This locust was not put off by the research that tells you the leaves of jatropha will not be conducive to a good night's sleep if you choose to eat them; this locust eats a whole plant.

And? I ask.

And nothing, that's it. It turned up, ate a plant and left.

So to my mind, what if he/she (I have no idea about the gender of a jatropha-eating locust) turns up the next night and eats another, or worse turns up with the family and friends: the crop could be gone in an instant! It didn't and it hasn't, but you never know do you!?

Next? Mildew. One Friday morning, mildew was spotted on 1 bush; by Friday evening it was on 60 bushes. I am told that had it been left, it would have affected the whole farm within 2 weeks. What if it hadn't been spotted, what if the farm manager was on holiday, what if there is a shortage of chemical spray, what if …?

The wrong kind of flowers

So now we turn our attention to the flowers, which eventually become seed. Why isn't this bush flowering?

We have a soil deficiency.
Is that a problem?
No, we can add fertilizer to make up for the deficiency.
So we do that; it makes no difference.
So why did it make no difference?
We bought organic fertilizer, and it hasn't germinated – or for those amongst us who aren't farmers, it hasn't broken down into the soil and had any impact. It's as though it's wrapped in little plastic bags, and nobody has opened the bags.
So we can buy other fertilizer?
Indeed.
Great!
We have a section treated with the new fertilizer, but we still have poor flowering.
Why? I ask.
These plants need nutrients sprayed to the leaves.
Of course, who wouldn't know that!?
We go to the next bush. There's loads of flowers, enough to export to Denmark!
That's great, I say.
Looking at our farm manager, I can tell it's not so great! And the reason? Not enough female flowers, or was it male flowers? I'm confused, and I'm slowly losing the will to live.

An invasion of ants
Next came: anthills.
Why are these a problem?
If you don't destroy them, they apparently will grow and grow and not stop growing, and slowly, like Triffids, will

eventually envelop the farm. At this point we had 62, all of them larger than a small van; they were significant and had all grown since we took occupation of the site.

And what are anthills? Well, as with bees, where you have a queen bee, with ants you have a queen ant, which tends to be white and the size of a football. OK, I exaggerate, perhaps the size of a tennis ball; but it's still a ball and bigger than something you might find in your shoe. This queen is the fertilizer, and from her all the babies are born; our queen is a busy little ant, given the size of the hills. To get rid of an anthill you have to kill the queen, otherwise she will just keep producing. Funnily enough, the hill is actually very fertile and can be good for the farm; once the queen is dealt with, the residue can be used as fertilizer, but if you just let the ant hills grow, they will destroy your land.

So, as we stand looking at the anthills and watch our workers tear into them, I spot a 7ft (or at least 6ft6in) snake lying dead on the ground. Yes, you guessed it: the snakes love to eat the ants, it's like an all-day breakfast for them. So as you destroy the ant hills, you also have to watch for the snakes.

Are they dangerous? I casually enquire, looking at this dead 7ft snake.

Oh no – you don't want to worry about them, it's those you want to worry about ...

As he says this, Urbanus, our farm manager, points to the biggest snake I have ever seen in my life – this time no exaggeration! If that one bites you, you will die before you get to hospital.

Then there's the electricity. We waited a couple of years to be connected, and as soon as we were connected, we were promptly disconnected for not paying the bill! But did we ever receive this bill?

For any of you non-farmers, can you understand how this venture alone would be enough for you never to sleep again?

A change of management
And then management is difficult when you are so far away. We had a farm manager who seemed good enough. Then something goes wrong, and you ask for an explanation. You want to believe him because you don't want to have misplaced your trust. So you continue to trust him, and something else goes wrong; you ask, you get an answer, and again your confidence is challenged, but you continue. This happens several more times, until eventually the evidence is too much to ignore. So we dismiss him. We are not entitled to pay any compensation by law, but he has worked with us for several years and the rights and wrongs of what he has done don't really matter as he goes home to his family without a job. Therefore, we pay him something to help, and a new manager is put in place.

On the farm we have our permanent workers and then casuals who we employ on a daily basis, at peak times. When our new manager takes over paying the casuals, the first person he pays says,

Oh, you have increased the rate!
No, the rate is unaltered; the previous manager had been skimming a little from everybody he employed. They are

hardly paid a significant rate in the first place, and despite the little they did have, the old manager was looking after himself first.

CONCLUDING THE CASE AGAINST JET ROVER FARM

A neighbouring farmer had a cow die and, we think, aware of the dangers to animals eating jatropha leaves, decided to sue us for negligence and compensation for the death of his cow. When the case came to court, it was against the 'Jet Rover Farm', which I must say was a far more exciting name.[32] Obviously, what the plaintiff had overlooked was that, although humans may not be able to sense that the leaves were dangerous to eat, his cow definitely would have done, and the case was thrown out.

∿∿∿∿∿∿∿∿∿∿∿∿∿∿∿∿∿∿∿∿∿∿∿

It is no wonder many investors won't touch agriculture. You are at the mercy of practically everything going wrong. In fact, the likelihood of everything going right is about as likely as you being hungry, praying for food and a roast duck flying into your mouth. To end the story, we never did get the yields to a consistent level, although we were going in the right direction. We were in discussions with an investor, who had experience of growing jatropha, to roll out the 2,000 acres, and they were confident we would get to the viable yields. But with the drop in the oil price, which

32 'Jatropha' sounds an awful lot like 'Jet Rover' in a Kenyan accent!

led to a lack of confidence in the market, we decided that the future was too unpredictable and we would close the farm.

As I conclude this chapter of my life, I can tell you that we sold the land and, literally as I write, the sale is being concluded. With the increase in land value it will compensate for a large percentage of our expenditure, but not 100%. We will pay back to our investors a % of their original investment. In total we only had four investors; one, from day 1, had written off the investment and was rather surprised when we told him we would be repaying him, one still loves us, one had transferred the investment as a gift to HiH charity and the remaining investor is still looking for me.[33]

And my conclusion is that it all made sense, and our goals were good. I reckon if the oil price had not dropped, we could have gone on to achieve our goals. On the other hand, some experts probably predicted the dip in oil prices which we didn't see coming. But as I have said before, there is no formula to business success, and if you don't try things, nothing will work.

---

33 Only kidding, he is actually a board member and remains as optimistic about HiHG as he always has been, although grateful that farming wasn't our only business.

POINTS TO PONDER

- If you are going into farming you should probably be a farmer.
- There is no finite list of what can go wrong when you are growing large scale.
- Agriculture is probably one of the highest risk investments.
- Know when to quit.

CHAPTER 10

NO BRIBES PLEASE, WE'RE PASTORS

or

DEALING WITH CORRUPTION AND EXPLOITATION

I was driving down Ngong Road in Nairobi in slow traffic, using my phone, when a police officer indicated for me to pull over. A bus was parked in the small lay-by, and a car was double-parked beside the bus. To avoid blocking the road, I drove past the 2 parked vehicles and pulled in by the kerb. The police officer banged the side of the car several times with whatever police officers hold in their hands, shouting at me to stop. I parked as I had intended, and got out of the car. The officer immediately took my phone, indicated for me to stand by the roadside and informed me that he was arresting me for 2 reasons:

1. Driving whilst using a cell phone.
2. Resisting arrest.

He then informed me that I would need to appear in court the following morning to answer the 2 charges. I acknowledged that I had been using my phone whilst driving; however, I had not resisted arrest, but simply manoeuvred the car to a safe location by the roadside instead of blocking the road. The police officer repeated the 2 offences for which I was being charged, reiterating that I would have to answer in court the following day. I repeated my admission and rejection, and confirmed I would attend court as requested.

The police officer then said that, alternatively, we could sort this out by the side of the road. If a police officer in the UK says that to you, he then writes out a fixed penalty and you pay on the spot – or so I am told. At first, I thought that was what the police officer meant. But that was not what he meant. What the officer meant was that, if I wanted to avoid court the next day, what was I prepared to offer him?

I told him that I was not prepared to offer anything; I had broken Kenyan law by using my phone whilst driving, I had not resisted arrest and I would appear in court the following day as the law determined. With that response, the police officer requested I get back in the car and then told my passenger (let's call him Bernard) to get out because the officer now wanted to speak with him. Bernard duly gets out, a few words are exchanged, Bernard returns to the car and tells me to drive off.

What happened there? I enquire.

Bernard explained,

> *I told the police officer that we were pastors and that we don't bribe, so to continue with the arrest. On hearing this, the police officer told us to move on.*

Now, we are not pastors, but Bernard felt it was easier to explain to a police officer that we were, as he would understand that better than explaining what a committed Christian is. You may take issue with that, but on balance it was OK with me. The following day I told the story to a Kenyan Indian friend, who listened with understanding and then responded,

It's all very well for you to claim the moral high ground, but when you get stopped by these guys twice a week, you cannot afford the time to go to court (you would probably lose the whole morning there, if not the day). It is easier, quicker and cheaper to sort it out by the side of the road.

Do you see his point?

SO IS IT *ALWAYS* WRONG?

On another occasion, I was driving to the airport for my return flight to the UK. There is very little that will stand in the way of me and the airport! I was stopped at a police checkpoint. I wound down the passenger window and a massive police man put his entire upper body through the window.

Police officer: *Good evening.*

Me: *Good evening.*

Police officer: *How are you tonight?*

Me: *Very fine, thank you.*

Police officer: *Where are you going?*

Me: *I am on the way to the airport.*

Police officer: *That's good, where are you flying to tonight?*

Me: *I'm flying home, I come from the UK.*

Police officer: *That's very nice, I hope you have a safe flight. Do you have anything for me?*

Me: *Are you asking for a bribe?*

Police officer: (*loud laughter*) *Have you done anything wrong?*

Me: *Not that I am aware of!*

Police officer: *Then how can I be asking you for a bribe? You haven't done anything wrong! You have more than me, and I'm just asking if you have anything for me.*

Me: (*not such loud laughter*) *Well fair play to you, clever response.*

So I gave him KES200 (about £1.50). Why? Because I did have more than him and he wasn't threatening my passage. He probably was abusing his uniform, and using a different set of words it would have been seen as a bribe, but perhaps he was smarter than the others, or he read my character. I'm not sure, but I did give him the money.

On another occasion, when driving at 120km/hr in a 100km/hr area, we are stopped by the police.

Police officer: *You were doing 120 in a 100 zone. Give me KES 5,000 (£35) and I'll let you go.*

My friend: *We are Christians; we are not into bribery, we are into forgiveness.*

Police officer: (*Slight sigh, pondering her options*) *OK, on your way.*

My friend: *We acknowledge that we were driving too fast, we acknowledge we broke the law, we acknowledge that you have forgiven us and so I would like to give you KES 1,000 (£7) to help feed your children.*

So who had the clever words this time? Are we playing the same game, just beating a different drum? Are my hands clean? Did we teach the police officer a moral lesson? Were we a testament to the God we profess to be in obedience to? I don't know, but she was probably KES 1,000 better off than she expected, having accepted we wouldn't bribe.

I am not suggesting interaction with corruption is simple. Some might try to make a distinction between giving and taking a bribe – and the more I think about it, the more I believe there can never be justification for a Christian *taking* a bribe, which has to mean taking advantage of those weaker than you and ultimately crushing either honesty, the poor or the weak. But as regards to paying bribes, or commissions, or introduction fees or 'thank yous' – depending on your culture – this area can be a lot harder. If you tender for construction work (anywhere in the world), you may *have* to pay a bribe to win a contract. If you don't bribe, you may have no contracts and you may become bankrupt.

JUST DON'T GO THERE?

Corruption is simply bad for business. In a survey of more than 350 businesses worldwide, 35% of companies have been deterred from an otherwise attractive investment opportunity because of the host country's reputation for corruption.[34] So do we move our business to where there is no bribery?

Many would say that the construction industry is corrupt the world over. I can only speak from my own experience,

34 John Bray, 'Facing up to Corruption: A practical business guide', *Control Risks* (Simmons & Simmons: 2007).

which as a young QS was fairly limited. At one point I was responsible for awarding a small sub-contract package for building miles of block walls. I had measured the Bill of Quantities[35] and sent it out to 3 tenderers. In relation to the £17m shopping mall that was constructed in Colchester, this was an insignificant package, although sizeable enough.

One of the tenderers rang to meet me on site, to which I agreed. He came down, we had a look and he then explained that his rate would be £9.00/m^2 plus £1 for me. Pretending that I was used to this sort of environment, I told the gentleman that he had got me wrong and the package would be let on the most competitive price, not to the person who paid me the most, and we parted company. As I walked back to the site office, I reflected on the conversation, thinking that, for all I was aware, some QSs were 'on the take'. I felt somewhat disappointed that he reckoned I could be bought off for £1. Let's face it, what could I have bought with £1? The minimum I would have expected would have been a small envelope. As I returned to my desk, I retold the story to my supervising QS, expressing my disappointment at the small buy-off figure, to which he and my fellow surveyors all erupted in laughter.

And the joke is? I indignantly enquired.

They then explained that I was being offered £1.00/m^2, and there were something like 23,000m^2 of block walls. I now felt better, and worse; worse for being naïve, better that at least I had turned down a decent bribe.

So don't think corruption is something that only happens 'over there' amongst 'those African people' while we folks in

---

35 A detailed statement of work, prices, dimensions and other details, for the erection of a building by contract.

the West look on, tutting with disdain. According to the National Fraud Authority, £48 billion is laundered through the UK every year (2% of UK GDP).[36] 'Be careful whilst you look at the spec of sawdust in your brother's eye whilst all the time there is a humongous plank sticking out of your own.'[37] This is a phrase we should not forget.

BUT WHY IS IT SO WRONG?

Some of you might be reading this and thinking,

> *So what? Why is Grant getting all agitated about corruption? Yes, we know it's a downside, but it's the system that has evolved and it actually works, in a fashion, so leave us alone and go back to the culture you understand.*

Poverty. Inequality. Broken public services. Politicians who serve themselves. Business owners who abuse their power. From India to Athens, from Wall Street to the Arab Spring – all over the world people are taking to the streets. Whilst their grievances are particular to each country, there remains a common thread throughout – corruption.

But what is corruption, exactly? I mean, where do we draw the line? Is it government ministers creaming the top off international deals, with funds that never reach the contractors it was intended for? Is it the poor police officer who doesn't get paid a living wage, and has to supplement his income from the streets? But then, if the politicians weren't corrupt, he could be paid a proper wage. So where did the corruption begin?

36 National Fraud Authority, 'Annual Fraud Indicator (AFI) Report, March 2012, https://assets.publishing. service.gov.uk/government/uploads/system/uploads/attachment_data/file/118530/annual-fraud-indica-tor-2012.pdf.

37 Matthew 7:5 and Luke 6:42, my paraphrase.

Here's a definition of corruption which I think sums it up well:

> *Corruption is the abuse of entrusted power for private gain. It hurts everyone whose life, livelihood or happiness depends on the integrity of people in a position of authority. Corruption holds back economic development, prevents a free market operating for businesses and consumers, and further exploits already marginalised groups.*[38]

Corruption hits the poorest hardest.

Corruption undermines authority

In Nairobi, a cheap and popular form of transport is the *matatu*, a 14-seater minibus, which operates on every possible route in and out of the city. Generally, a *matatu* has a driver and a conductor who takes the fares. If they do get paid a wage, it seems they can enhance it by getting as many people on the *matatu* as possible and by completing each route as quickly as possible, so that they can complete more journeys in a day. The result is that *matatu* drivers are notorious. They drive as fast as they can, cut up other drivers whenever they can and stop whenever they like. They drive wherever they can; it doesn't matter if it's a road, the pavement, the forecourt of a petrol station, somebody's front garden, the central reservation, the opposite carriageway, through trees – just about anywhere they can physically make their minibus go. I haven't seen a *matatu* in a

38 'Introduction: Why fight corruption?', *Global Citizen*, https://www.globalcitizen.org/en/content/introduction-why-fight-corruption/ (Accessed 21 February 2019).

shopping mall yet, but I am sure the day is coming!

And why can they drive like this? Because the police have lost all authority due to the constant lining of their own pockets. Everybody knows it goes on; nobody does anything to stop it. Because of the way *matatu* drivers drive, other drivers get frustrated, and now, increasingly drive the same way. The consequence? You are now more likely to die in a traffic accident in Kenya than from malaria.

And if you're thinking that is a triumph for beating malaria, forget it.

You see, few people like authority. Many of us wouldn't confess to having a traffic warden as a friend, and who would want to be a football referee? (Some actually do, I know, but I wouldn't.) And as for Health and Safety Inspectors, I am sure they are referees at the weekend. But these 3 roles are in place to enforce the rules so that we can all co-exist in harmony. In Romans 13:1, Paul encourages us to submit to authority because there is no authority other than that given by God. Sometimes we may struggle to understand that, especially when we witness oppressive authorities, but this is Paul's instruction and to ignore it is to turn our back on the word of God.

Corruption costs lives

Some of these are light-hearted examples, but the truth is serious. On the anniversary of Haiti's devastating earthquake, Roger Bilham calculated that 83% of all deaths from building collapse in earthquakes over the past 30 years occurred in countries that are institutionally corrupt.[39] Corruption in the building industry in particular puts people's lives at risk. Regulations are not adhered to, corners are cut and, ultimately, people die.

There are many levels of corruption, and unless it stops, it will continue to strangle and kill. Corruption is greed that kills. It is strangling economies, stunting investment and keeping the poor *poor*. If we excuse ourselves, thinking that whether we take or give a bribe won't make any difference, I'd say we need to think again, because all corruption starts at this point and grows from there.

Corruption, exploitation and oppression

In Kenya, the minimum wage is KES 9,000 (£65) per month. Somebody I know works in manufacturing on Mombasa Road for KES200 (£1.50) per day. If he says anything, he is out of a job; if he complains, he is out of a job; if he refuses to be paid such a ridiculously low wage, he is out of a job; and if he refuses to do the job, tomorrow, someone else will take his job.

I have another friend whose mother used to operate a sewing machine for similar wages. They stitched designer labels into jeans and sold them as the real thing. This was in the days when sewing machines were operated by your feet. This lady could work for about 10 days, then her feet would swell up so much that she would have to have 4 days off for her feet to recover. She was already on a pathetic wage, but due to the condition of her feet, she was probably reducing her wage by a further $^1/_3$. Consequently, she couldn't afford education for her son, so at a young age he was sent out on the streets to fend for himself.

39 Roger Bilham, 'Lessons from the Haiti earthquake', *Nature Vol 463*, 18 February 2010.

It's just wrong

Ultimately the reason for not bribing, and not receiving a bribe, for dealing fairly and truthfully in business is because corruption – and every form of lying, greed and selfishness – is behaviour that is incompatible with our life in Christ. Our Lord is truth; truth is integral to his character and he shines the light of his truth into our lives.[40] The experience of many Christians is that, as we follow the Holy Spirit into all truth and invite him to shine the light of truth into every part of our lives (including our work), lies become deeply uncomfortable – anathema to us. How can we be in Christ and participate in these things?

When we read the Bible, there is much to support this view. We are called not to store up treasure on earth and we learn that greed is, in fact, idolatry. We learn that those who are thieves, who are greedy or who cheat people will not inherit the Kingdom of God.[41] In fact, God *hates* unfair dealing in business, and promises to bring justice to the oppressed.[42] The story of Ananias and Sapphira,[43] who sold land and then lied to the church about the price they received for it, is a sobering read, as are the warnings in the book of James to the rich, specifically about withholding payment from the poor.[44]

There are so many scriptures that we could quote that indicate God's view of laziness, exploitation and corruption, but a particular favourite of mine is Proverbs 6:6–15:

40 'I am the way and the truth and the life.' John 14:6.
41 See Matthew 6:19; I Corinthians 6:9–10; Ephesians 5:5; Colossians 3:5.
42 Psalm 10:18; Proverbs 11:11.
43 Acts 5:1–11.
44 James 5:1–6.

Go to the ant, you sluggard;
 Consider its ways and be wise!
It has no commander,
 no overseer or ruler,
yet it stores its provisions in summer
 and gathers its food at harvest.

How long will you lie there, you sluggard?
 When will you get up from your sleep?
A little sleep, a little slumber,
 a little folding of the hands to rest –
and poverty will come on you like a thief
 and scarcity like an armed man.

A troublemaker and a villain,
  who goes about with a corrupt mouth,
  who winks maliciously with his eye,
  signals with his feet
  and motions with his fingers,
  who plots evil with deceit in his heart –
  he always stirs up conflict
Therefore disaster will overtake him in an instant;
  he will suddenly be destroyed – without remedy.

We are created in God's image, and God is a Creator God who has given us work: a gift from him. And so we gain a just sense of satisfaction from creating something, from achievement, rather than money itself. A lazy person, someone who does not work, may not have that sense of achievement and may feel dissatisfied. There is a perception that money makes you happy and that giving in to bribery makes life easier, but I want to challenge that view. I want to try and demonstrate that it is Christ who motivates me, and that money genuinely doesn't. I want to bring a wholesome witness, to reflect the fullness of life in Christ. Under the table dealings, giving an advantage to one person because you can, leaving the poor disadvantaged and powerless – that to me does not seem to reflect the image of God in my life, nor a temple for God living in me. Ultimately, I don't think this is a cultural choice.

Don't get me wrong: there are corrupt practices in the UK, and there are probably corrupt practices all over the world; but I don't really work in the UK, nor all over the world. I work in Kenya, and this is my response in a setting which I think I understand a bit about.

So, how can we respond?

With prayer.

STRATEGIES

Thinking on your feet
But there are sometimes other things we can do. Whilst working on the project with the block walls, I was responsible for the floor screeder's package.[45] The package was one of the last to be awarded and had to take place at the end of the project. The floor screeder's QS was a retired man who had gone freelance, who did all his measurements

45 Floor screed is a cementitious material used in construction.

to 3 decimal places. He was completely straightforward, honest and I got on well with him. He submitted his 3rd valuation. My job was to check his valuation and then make a recommendation for payment, which was then signed off by my surveying director. The surveying director only visited the site every Wednesday, which mean that we junior surveyors all prepared our accounts for signing off by Tuesday night.

On Wednesday morning I see Richard (name changed to protect the guilty) and ask him to sign off the payment. His response,

No.

Why? I enquire.

Because the project has run out of money and you will have to find some excuse not to pay.

But there is no reason not to pay, I respond.

He told me to grow up; there are 'always reasons not to pay.'

I leave Richard's office and hear my phone ringing: it's the floor screeder's QS asking when they are going to get paid. What do I say now? My instructions from the people that employ me are to find a reason not to pay, but I have no reason, and there is no reason, so what do I say now?

What colour shirt are you wearing?

Yellow, why?

Ah ha: there is my reason for not paying; we are not paying anyone wearing yellow shirts this week.

This would have made as much as sense as any other excuse I could come up with. Thinking on my feet, I suggested that he come to see me the following Wednesday.

I can, but when are you paying us? he asked.

Just come to site next Wednesday, I responded.

Confused, he put the phone down.

Next Wednesday at 8am, he turns up on site. I politely show him into the meeting room and leave. I then knock on Richard's door and explain that the floor screeders are here to see him.

What do I want to see the floor screeders for? I have nothing to say to them. Richard rather dismissively responded.

I replied,

Well, you told me not to pay them, but I haven't got a reason, so you had better tell them yourself, because I am not lying for you.

Reluctantly Richard goes to the meeting room. About 10 minutes later he returns, slams the payment certificate on my desk and, in a rather unfriendly tone in my opinion, tells me to pay them.

You see Richard, I said, *it is easy for you to hide behind me to tell someone you won't pay them, but it's a different matter when you have to tell them yourself.*

STANDING YOUR GROUND – EVEN WHEN IT HURTS

We are building houses in Kenya. We buy a large piece of land, build houses and then register the plot for subdivision in order to give the buyer title of their property. Before you can register the land title, the council has to issue an occupation certificate. For an occupation certificate a representative from the council has to come and inspect the property. We have 50 units ready for inspection. The inspector comes to visit and informs us that the certificates may take a few weeks. However, if we paid her £350, the certificates would be issued the following day.

In order to build these houses, we have finance from the bank. Our finance is costing us £600 per day. What do you do? As directors, we were united on the principle that we don't give into such evil; but it really doesn't make any economical business sense! In the end, it took 2 months to get the completion certificates.

My ultimate conclusion and experience is that, no matter what corrupt practices are put in our way to prevent us from achieving our aims, if we are patient, faithful and persistent, we will break through the selfish greed of petty officers looking to line their own pockets. It will always cost more than the bribe in loss of time, or inefficiencies or delayed returns, but we will always get there.

So for Kenya, which is really all I know, when you're looking at corruption in the headlights, you fasten your seat belt, pray for wisdom and patience, and commit yourself to defeating this evil. In time you know it will give way, because ultimately the bribe-seeker will get bored and move onto another vulnerable target.

~~~~~~

POINTS TO PONDER

- Corruption at its simplest deprives the poor.
- Don't think it is purely an African problem; it is happening in the UK possibly just as much.
- Can involvement in corruption be compatible with the Spirit of the Lord living in you?
- Kenyan police officers went to their own special academy!

~~~~~~

PS: THE OTHER SIDE OF THE COIN

My Kenyan friends tell me that you can't be fully Kenyan until you have attended a *harambe*, a wedding and a funeral. (Which I know sounds like the name of a film.) A *harambe* is a community fundraiser, when family, friends and neighbours come to together to raise money for a particular purpose. I have been to a *harambe*. I'm sure you all know what a wedding is, and I have enjoyed a few of those in Kenya. Thus far, I have not attended a Kenyan funeral. And so some would say I am $^2/_3$ Kenyan.

I have subsequently discovered there is a 4th criterion: being accused of corruption. By the revised calculation, I have recently increased my Kenyan nationality status to $^3/_4$.

Many people's perspective of Kenya is that you can't do business unless you are prepared to bribe. It is not true. So far in my business life, I can tell you we have never bribed, or authorized a bribe; and we have not been prevented from carrying out business. Interestingly, we have also never been offered a bribe, which I hope is testimony to our reputation that it would not be accepted.

Where shall I begin? I was invited onto the board of a university in Kenya, which had, and has, an outstanding reputation as a Christian institution. One of the disciplines at the university was business, and one of the reasons I was invited onto the board was to bring my understanding of how you apply learned business skills from the classroom to the real world. The real world where people are lining their pockets and you suddenly have to act with integrity and apply ethics in an environment which has forgotten how to spell such words.

In addition to the university having a council to which I had been invited, there was also a commercial company which sat alongside the university. The purpose of the commercial company was to undertake commercial activity, make a profit and contribute said profit to the university. Having become a board member, it was logical for me to be invited to join the commercial company. From my perspective there were 2 purposes of the company:

1. To create an additional income stream to the university.
2. To operate as an example to business students of what clean ethical business looks like.

One potential business I could see for the company was to rent out buildings and space when the university was not utilizing it. I had recently attended my son's graduation at a UK university and had noted that a significant percentage of their income came from renting out idle space; I saw no reason why the same principle couldn't be applied at other universities.

There are few areas in which I consider myself to be an expert, but regarding this, I have actually managed a similar enterprise in the UK. The offices of HiH are in a converted barn; there are 10 offices, 3 are occupied by HiH and the remainder are rented out to other tenants. The barn is owned by a charitable trust, of which the trustees are myself and 2 members of the original farm. So HiH manage the barn, we set aside funds for maintenance and improvements, and 100% of the resulting profit is allocated to charitable work known to the trustees. The concept for the university was therefore very similar and, to my mind, quite achievable.

I subsequently sat down and worked out the total facilities available in just one of the university buildings. As typical for a cash flow, I looked at the best and worst case scenarios and considered that this could be a very lucrative business for the university. The building in question was a new construction, had some modern facilities and was close to town. The downside was access to sufficient parking, but, to be fair, there are very few venues in Nairobi that don't have a parking challenge.

We therefore drew up an MoU between HiH and the university to implement my plans. I considered that it would not be right to expose the university to financial risk;

consequently, the MoU outlined that HiH would invest in the marketing of the building. If we made a profit, we would contribute to the university. If we never achieved the income which had been forecast and if, in fact, the project never moved into profit and ran at a loss, that financial liability lay 100% with HiH. Making that proposal, I didn't see how we could not be successful. It wasn't as if we were saddled with the financing of the construction: the university had taken care of that themselves. I figured that all we needed to do was to employ an effective marketing officer and an additional accountant to count the money coming in.

I appreciate that any business person who has just walked in off the street and read this will be thinking,

What kind of businessman are you? You share in the risk, you share in the profit, you don't load the dice fully in your client's favour!

I can see your point, but I considered the risk to be minimal and we were only doing this for the benefit of the university, so even if it did cost HiH, we didn't want the university to lose out.

Well, I won't bore you with the details of a flattened economy due to the election, and people being a little cautious about visiting Kenya because of the election, and businesses being cautious in their spending as they were concerned about the outcome of the elections. I won't go into any of that. But 18 months after signing the MoU, unbelievable as it may sound – and totally unpredicted by me and, come to that, totally unpredicted by anyone else – the project was still in deficit and had not moved into profit by a single cent, or shilling or penny (depending on what language you think in). HiH was carrying the cost of the investment, we were paying to the University a services charge on the rent we were achieving, but the project was in loss. (You will recall I mentioned a few sentences back that any loss or cost sat firmly with HiH and was of no liability to the university.)

It slowly became evident that other people in the university couldn't believe it had gone wrong either. It began as a low rumble, a bit like when you can see a thunderstorm in the distance: the clouds gather and you hear a noise like your stomach would appreciate having some input. But very quickly the clouds gathered overhead, the thunder cracked and the storm began. Basically, because nobody could believe that we hadn't made money, the following was said:

The university hasn't received any profit, but the project must have been making money so Smith must have put it in his socks and taken it back to the UK where we can't get our hands on it.

I can understand this viewpoint: I couldn't believe my plan hadn't worked, so I can understand that people who didn't know me wouldn't believe it either. Another unfortunate factor was that, at the same time, there were some other allegations that were being levelled at some other people in the university; the timing wasn't helpful. I was then included in an independent investigation into the various allegations which were floating around – my handling of the rental income being one. This I welcomed, because I was convinced that HiH and myself would be found innocent of any charge and HiH would be left to continue making a loss, or hopefully turn the project round into profit.

The investigation got underway, I was interviewed (as were many others) and the report of the findings was released. I should just add in here for context, that by this time my two terms as a board member had been completed and I was no longer a member of the board.[46]

Back to the investigation: their report was submitted to the board, but there was a significant delay in releasing it to people like myself. Obviously, this was a little concerning because, if it was straightforward, it would have been released straight away. When I did eventually receive a copy, I realized that, just as I couldn't believe we had lost money on this 'dead cert' business, and just as those who made allegations in my direction couldn't believe the project had lost money, the investigators couldn't believe it either. I was therefore found guilty. However, it got worse in that there were some new allegations, which I hadn't even heard of, which had been thrown into the mix, and I was found guilty of these too.

It was at this point that I realized that, within this Christian institution, there were a few who had their knives out and that some of those knives were pointed at me. At the time I responded to every allegation against HiH and myself. However, I continued to be in the position where neither had I been confirmed guilty nor exonerated of the allegations.

---

46 Every Board member served 2 terms of 3 years. If you are wondering how the project had only been running 18 months, but 6 years has expired, it's because I didn't immediately become a member of the commercial company and I didn't immediately implement the renting-out project.

As somebody said to me when this was all going on,

The problem you have, is that nobody has met any businessman who has the interests of the university first and their own interests second. Everybody would assume you are out to feather your own nest first, and if there was any benefit to the university, that would be an added bonus!

Because the truth is, for many and various reasons (some which are known to me and some which are not) HiH actually failed to turn a fantastic resource into a profit, but I am sure few people associated with the university will believe that.

My biggest concern was that the reputation of HiH – the charity and the business – that had been built up over 20 years, could be destroyed. I was concerned that, despite supporting 1000s of children, our reputation could be smeared, which ultimately would impact the children we supported. I would love to say that I am a strong character and none of this affected me, but of course that would not be the whole truth. Because while those close to you may know that you are innocent, there are many more who don't know you so well and will believe that there is no smoke without fire. And then there are those who are happy to listen to idle stories, to join in and perpetuate your guilt, and who probably genuinely believe the lies and continue to spread them. So I would feel angst over the injustice of my position.

Every now and again, generally when I was in church or praying with Sue, I would get to the point where I basically had to hand everything over to God. I had to acknowledge that God knew HiH's reputation and God didn't solely rely on me to defend it, that the accusations were no surprise to God and at some point we would all come out the other side. Then as I thought about my own position, I realized that Jesus was accused of being a criminal and died a criminal's death, was spat and jeered at and that most of the disciples ultimately died because of their faith. I concluded,

What right do I have to stand on my own moral high ground?

So on those days when I felt that angst, I would make a conscious decision to let go and put the injustices and our reputation at the foot of the cross. Of course, the problem with that decision is that after a couple of days, I would be amazed by yet another ridiculous and hurtful statement and pick the problem up again.

Now, the situation has been resolved, I have been exonerated and the parties concerned have confirmed my innocence, privately and publicly. But it took some time, and it is only by God's grace that I came through with the determination to continue investing in the work we have been doing. As I sit in my chair writing, I still strongly believe in the mission and vision of the university. I still firmly believe that the majority of faculty and staff share that mission and vision and act in a God-honouring way in all they say and do. But as I continue to reflect on my experiences of just a few people who call themselves Christians in both Kenya and the UK, I have come to the realization even more strongly that to be a disciple of Jesus Christ, it is the response of the heart that matters, and nobody else actually knows that true response. This, in my mind, is the only true evidence of who we are, and only we and God know it, and sometimes I am not even sure that we know.

But as I continue to reflect on my experiences of just a few people that call themselves Christians in both Kenya and the UK, I have come to the conclusion that we can:

- speak rousing sermons,
- be in the right place at 10am on a Sunday morning,
- give from our finances,
- get baptized,
- work for a Christian institution,
- lift up 'holy' hands whilst singing,
- fall down,
- sit on church committees,
- takes notes in sermons.

All of this can be completely meaningless. But to be a disciple of Jesus Christ, it is the response of the heart that matters, and nobody else actually knows that true response. This, in my mind, is the only true evidence of who we are, and only you and God know; sometimes I am not even sure that we know.

In my walk with God – over 40 years – I have met many people who say they are Christian, but sometimes that is in fact a lie, and practically every time that lie has become obvious, money is involved.

As Corrie Ten Boom said,
A mouse in the cookie jar isn't a cookie.[47]

47 Cited in Deborah Howard, *Sunsets: Reflections for Life's Final Journey* (Crossway Books: 2005), p.31.

POINTS TO PONDER:

- Don't assume that because you are involved with a Christian institution, that everybody – including you – will automatically behave like Jesus.
- If your friend is accused of something you don't understand, pick up the phone and find out their perspective.
- Don't let a few disappointing eggs deflect from the greater good.

CHAPTER 11

A WASTE PAPER BIN AT EUSTON STATION

or

ABOUT THE MONEY ...

So where was the money for the business to come from? If we were to do anything at all, we needed to find some investment. Which, for most of us, is the biggest question of all. And I have left it until now for a good reason.

What I have been trying to say throughout these pages is that, if I can do it, anyone can. You may be thinking you wouldn't know where to go to find investment, but nor did I. You may be thinking you wouldn't know how to structure an investment: nor did I. You may be wondering who would invest large amounts of money in your ideas: so did I. You may be thinking you'd have difficulty sleeping at night if you were handling millions of pounds of investment – actually I have never thought that, because ... well, I'm not sure why.

This chapter is about how we have found investment. Quite a lot of it. None of it was planned, but we didn't turn our backs on opportunity either. Because, as I said before, quantity surveyors count things. And they charge a lot.

~~~~~~~~~~~~~~~~~~~~~~~~~~~~~~~~~~

Our first investors were Peter and Jack. I am sure some people would say that the reason I invited them to the board was because of their money. To be fair, that isn't an unreasonable accusation, but it actually isn't the case. I invited them for their expertise and input; their investment was a subsequent bonus, if a little ironic – board members ought to get a reward out of the business rather than having to pay for the privilege!

Meet Tim

It was a lovely summer's day and we had been invited to a friend's wedding. At the reception, we found ourselves sitting next to Tim and Ruth, a couple unknown to us previously. Conversation flowed easily and 3 hours later we said our goodbyes. Sunday afternoon, I got an email from Tim saying,

Hi Grant, it was really nice to meet you and Sue yesterday. I was interested in what you do and wondered if you would like to meet up sometime.

I was a little surprised, but always keen to talk about what I do. For somebody to go to the effort of contacting me would tend to suggest that they would like to support us in some way. I thought that perhaps I should learn a little more about Tim, so I rang our wedding hosts,

Sue and I met Tim and Ruth at your wedding, we got on nicely, and today I received an email from Tim saying

he would like to meet up. Could you tell me a little more about them?
Friend: *Tim and Ruth live at the bottom of our road, my wife knows them more than me: 'school gate' talk, their granddaughter goes to school with our daughter. Tim is a businessman and was kind enough to lend us his car to bring the bridesmaids to the wedding.*
Me: *That would be the Bentley?*

We arrange to meet, picking up where we left off on the Saturday. Tim asks more about what we do and I explain the work of the charity. Tim listens intently and responds by telling me he has set up a trust fund and he would like to give some money to the charity. Tim goes on to explain that one project of the trust is to support 3 primary schools in Swaziland. From these 3 schools the fund then supports 12 students from each school to go to secondary school.

Bearing in mind our relationship is only a few hours old and this man has obviously taken an interest in what we do and would like to support our charity, I decide to do something next which, even I confess, is a bit risky:

Me: *Tim, would you like to get involved with the business?*
Tim: *Not at all.*
Me: *Why's that then?*
Tim: *I have been involved in business for 40 years and now I am moving out of it. I don't want any more involvement in business, I just want to give some money away.*
It is very rare for anyone to turn away a potential gift to the charity they feel passionate about. However, I wanted to ask another question:

Me: *Tim you were telling me about the 12 students from the 3 Swaziland primary schools; what happens to them after they go to secondary school? Do they just go and get a job?*

Tim: *No, it's not as easy as that; unemployment is very high in Swaziland and it is very difficult to get work.*

Me: *Oh, I see. Then, I wonder why you're interested in pouring thousands of pounds into education, but you're not interested in investing in jobs which could change a youngster's life permanently?*

A silence follows as Tim looks at me, and frankly I am not sure what I should do next!!

Perhaps I should just shake his hand and say,

Well it was nice knowing you briefly, where's the door?

Although, to be fair, the last bit would be an attempt at politeness, because I could see where the door was without asking.

Tim draws breath to end the uneasy silence. Which was an encouraging sign, because often when people are angry they forget to breathe, which of course would make things even worse.

And then he says,

I take your point, what are your ideas?

Tim subsequently invested £50k in HiH business and made donations to the charity. The investment was unrestricted, in as much as Tim wasn't being prescriptive about how we should spend it, but was keen to be kept updated on what we were doing. HiH had never had that type of money invested in us before. It was a big step. Basically, Tim was not investing in a business concept, he was expressing his belief and support of an organization that he considered had the capacity to deliver what it promised: namely, profitable business which was creating employment in Africa and paying people properly.

Now, meet Bob
At the same time as this happened, I had started talking to Bob. Bob and I had had a couple of chats about the business and he was expressing an interest in getting involved – primarily as an investor looking for a financial return, but also believing in the cause of HiH and supporting the work that we had been doing. It was also at this time that I had been contemplating how I could work full time at the Kenyan business. With that in mind, and thinking through how I could get Bob to finance my salary so I could give all my attention to Kenyan business, I had a lunch date with Bob with a view to bringing this subject up, hoping his response would be,

I'll pay your salary, buy you a car, a private jet and finance an office for the next 20 years.

Instead, his response was,

You really need to throw yourself into it.

What, with no salary, planes, cars or office??

Bob was prepared to consider committing investment in jatropha and the construction company. So we decided to travel to Kenya together to look at some options. This was around the time when Kenya erupted during the elections; the picture on our UK TV screens was basically one of Kenya imploding. Despite this, Bob travelled there with me in February 2008. Initially, I had identified a 0.6-acre prime plot for consideration, but we looked at various other land options whilst we were there. There was a particularly attractive 23-acre piece of land and there was also the possibility of an adjacent 10-acre piece of land. We had discussions with potential partners, we talked with our lawyer, we talked with Joshua. By the time we were flying home, it seemed as though the 23 acres could be a goer, but it didn't look like the adjacent 10 acres would happen.

Waiting for our departure, both feeling a little disgruntled that the additional 10 acres was not going to happen, I reflected: we had gone to Kenya to look at 0.6 of an acre, and were now involved in securing 23 acres, that was a pretty significant step!

Once we were home, Bob reflected on our visit and what he had seen and then requested we meet up. He was very optimistic about the potential and what HiH could do. He consequently was prepared to commit £300k to HiH. In order to attempt to get some cash for HiH running costs, we agreed a % that HiH would take from the investment, basically for allowing Bob to invest. Yes, you read that correctly, HiH were taking a % to allow Bob the privilege of investing, then on completion, HiH would take an additional % of any investment profit.

In the meantime, we formed a project Joint Venture company with a Kenyan partner with a view to constructing 200 houses. The JV would be a 50:50 company between the partner and HIH, with both companies putting in equal finances. It was anticipated we required about £800k investment, split 50:50. We decided to commit £200k of Bob's cash, we had another £100k from another investor; we therefore required a further £100k from another source.

Then there is Graham

A very smart investor: Graham invests in the business, but the return from his investment is going to go into HiH charity to fund a project that he is already personally funding. So no pressure there then, except if the business fails him, the project doesn't get the funding. That's what you call 'clever'.

FUNDING FOR JATROPHA

HiH NRG Ltd, was, as you will remember, the UK Investment company that raised money to invest in jatropha. We had a small round of funding and were now going for the second round. We approached several institutions that we thought would be interested in our business. This resulted in several visits to the City, arranging meetings, getting encouraging responses, but nobody committing investment. I guess the unanswered questions outweighed the social benefit and the financial risk which was perfectly understandable.

I was due to speak at a men's breakfast one Saturday morning at 7.30am. As the date got closer and I began to prepare my talk, I started to think,

Who wants to get out of bed for a breakfast at 7.30 on a Saturday morning to listen to me?

I didn't want to do the talk any more, suffering from a case of the grumps, feeling all sorry for myself for having to go to the breakfast and sorry for those who had to listen to me.

But I went, and so did about 35 other men. I spoke about the business, about the housing and about the farm. At the end, a gentleman with a HiHT brochure in his hands (which has a fact sheet about jatropha inside) came and spoke to me, asking for more info. Still suffering from the grumps, I was a little dismissive, saying that if he wanted to know more, he should visit the Internet. His response was that he would be in touch. Yes, I thought, and I will fly to the moon for lunch and be back in time for the 3pm kick off.

So it will be no surprise to you that in the afternoon I received an email, inviting me to his home to discuss more about the jatropha business. I went to see him, and found out that this man managed a trust fund and was interested in us. This is what happened next:

Potential investor: *How much investment are you looking for?*

Me: £200k

Potential Investor: *If we invested £100k, would you find the other £100k in Kenya?*

Me: *Probably not, although in construction that was the original financing arrangement, i.e., 50:50 financing from UK and Kenya. With the jatropha, our partners were more responsible for managing day to day and HiHNRG were responsible for raising investment. However, when you are looking for such a sum, once you have half of it, the other half is always easier to find.*

Potential Investor: *OK, is there anything else I can invest in?* He obviously didn't know me very well! That's like saying to a child,

Would you like some chocolate?

The meeting concluded with the investor saying that he would discuss with his accountant and come back to us.

Leaving the meeting, I felt cautiously optimistic. Listening to my messages there was one from Sue,

You know that tree at the bottom of the garden you said would never fall down?

It's fallen down!

Life is an interesting mix. A few days later £100k investment was confirmed in jatropha.

Henry

I had joined a group called Transformational Business Network (TBN). TBN were holding a conference, which included a speaker who had an investment fund for East Africa. I had decided to go to the conference with Neil. My motive for attending the conference was to meet the speaker with the fund and see if we could do something together. As we gathered, registered and drank coffee, Neil and I chatted:

Neil: *I have just prayed*

Me: *Great, what about?*

Neil: *If God wants HiH to work with this guy who you have come to see, he will come to speak to us, rather than us going up to him. If he doesn't come to us, God doesn't want us to have a relationship with him.*

Me: *Oh.*

There are about 200 delegates at the conference and 4 or 5 speakers. At events like this, everyone wants to talk to the speakers, so the likelihood of one of them coming to speak to us is about as likely as a roast turkey flying in through the window at Christmas, complete with stuffing and garnished with roast potatoes. However, I respect Neil, and that was his prayer.

The morning progresses with stimulating topics, and then lunch. Lunch is a buffet where you help yourself, then go and sit at a table. Neil and I collect our lunch, sit down at a table and the conference organizer comes over and says,

This year we are having themed tables, so people can go to a table where there is a topic being discussed that is of particular interest to them. Who would you like to have come and sit at your table?

Neil: *Matey boy with the East African Investment fund.*

Duly, the conference organizer put's Henry's name on our table. As people collect their food, those that want to speak to Henry come to our table; Henry comes to our table and discussion commences. As lunch draws to a close, people leave our table until there is only Henry, Neil and I left. Henry then enquires,

So what do you guys do?

It turned out that the next time I was planning to be in Nairobi would coincide with when Henry, also, would be in Nairobi; we arranged to meet for breakfast. There was no further communication between us until then. Henry's wife was also at the breakfast, and we talked about HiH business and the fact that we were looking for £100k to complete our share of the investment in the 200-unit housing project. Henry asked his wife what she thought. Her response was,

HiH's fees seem extortionate.

To which Henry replied,

Yes, they are, but I like them!

Henry invested the £100k.

Once back in the UK, Henry requested that we send the paperwork through for him to sign. Paperwork!? Everybody else had just transferred bank to bank; paperwork was a new concept! I assumed by 'paperwork' that he was requesting some kind of contract, so I put a 4-page document together and sent it. Henry called me.

Henry: *Grant, this is hardly a legal document, is it?*

Me: *No, I just tried to capture the essence of our agreement.*

Henry: *OK, I guess we could both employ expensive lawyers and ultimately just come up with a document that means the same.*

Obviously I agreed, although I didn't know any expensive lawyers.

Henry: *OK, I'll sign it, but I would like to add a clause.*

Me: *Yep, what would that be?*

Henry: *Basically that you declare that you have told me the truth.*

Me: *No problem, add it at the end.*

Duly the document was returned signed, with an added piece in Henry's hand writing that I declared that the above information was, to the best of my knowledge, the truth. Henry then went on to say that he would leave the money in a waste paper bin at Euston Station.

And Henry accused *me* of being unprofessional?!

The dragons' den

One day the phone rings. It's an investor enquiring how things are going. As the conversation progresses the investor asks where HiH would like to go next, to which I respond that we currently actually had on the table an offer for a 100-acre piece of land and, if we bought that, it would set us up for years. The response of the investor was,

Investor: *How much money would you need to purchase the land?*

Me: *About £1m.*

Investor: *I think we could do that for you.*

The problem is these statements are all made with good intention. Having had so many remarkable experiences with investors – some, frankly, verging on the unbelievable – I have come to understand that God has a bigger sense of humour than me, and so I take every statement seriously.

There were obviously some conditions to this investment, and these conditions included:

- Terms of finance
- Equity share in the company
- Exclusivity
- Due diligence
- Business plan
- Subordination documents
- Bond account
- Me giving up UK surveying

It was becoming apparent that a handshake and a 4-page agreement were no longer going to suffice. Nobody likes giving away a share of their company; if you watch the TV programme *Dragons' Den*, they come on asking for £1m for 0.05% share in their company and they either walk away with nothing, or £1m having given away 99% of the company. Of course any investor reading this would say that the term 'given away' is wrong, it should be considered as 'sharing' a % of the company. But given that you never see that % again, I think it is more accurate to say 'given away'.

We didn't actually have too much of a problem with that bit, although I will always try and negotiate down the %. I recall saying to the investors,

This is a large %.

To which they responded,

We are taking on a large risk.

Which is fair. Even the business plan suggested by this investor was achievable and, of course, me giving up UK surveying had already been on the agenda for some time. The clause we had a problem with was exclusivity.

Basically what was being requested was that HiH would only receive finance from this investor. This meant that if we wanted to grow faster than this investor wanted us to grow, or if we wanted to get involved in a business this investor wasn't interested in, HiH wouldn't be able to do it. Giving away a % is hard enough when you are an innovative, creative, ideas person, and to be told where you can go and how fast you can go there is not appealing. To look at it from the investors' point of view, you can also see their perspective: if we suddenly had access to finance a polar bear sanctuary in the North Pole with an investment of £100m, would HiH still give as much attention to the £1m investment in a piece of land in Kenya?

We continued to talk over a period of time, and eventually came to terms with most of their requirements. I had even started to wind down my UK surveying activities. Our one sticking point was exclusivity.

On Thursday 15 April, Rick, Emma and I set out for a meeting to conclude the deal. Rick is on the HiH management board and Emma, as you will remember, was my PA. We were confident that, having got this far, a deal would be struck. Everything is negotiable. The skill of doing a business deal is simply ensuring that both parties get most of what they want. Although having said that 'everything is negotiable', as we travel up on the train we agree between us that, for us, the exclusivity clause, as it stands, is our one non-negotiable.

We settle down to the meeting and launch into our discussion. Rick decides to go for the non-negotiable from the beginning and within about 20 minutes, it becomes clear that exclusivity is not up for discussion. We spend a further $2^1/_2$ hours explaining our standpoint and then it is suggested that we take 30 minutes to ourselves and then reconvene.

The investors leave the room, the 3 of us are left looking at each other, all of one mind. We said we couldn't accept exclusivity, and we won't. There is no discussion; we are unanimous. We are also pretty convinced that, while everything is negotiable, as long as only one side says they won't negotiate, you can still be on track. We were, however, fairly certain that the investor wasn't going to budge either. So having been convinced that a deal was there to be done, the reality starts to dawn on us that it isn't going to happen. We now sit for 29 minutes and wait for the investor's team to come back. Rick has other appointments, so leaves Emma and I to bear the bad news to the investor. The investors return, we give our response and receive the anticipated reaction.

We tidy up our papers, close our laptops and prepare to leave.

At that point the investor then puts another option on the table, taking away the % and the exclusivity. There are obviously conditions, but our main sticking point has been removed. Our discussions therefore continue and move on to due diligence in Nairobi.

Going through due diligence for HiH was a completely new experience and rather a daunting one, not because we had anything to hide, but just because we had never jumped through such hoops before. But we passed – as is to be expected! Over the next 3 months, documents went backwards and forwards, alterations were made in the way that only lawyers can alter documents, papers were signed and, eventually, the funds were transferred to HIH.

Over the years, I have met many investors. Most investors have agendas, and, you may be surprised to know, they aren't always looking purely at a financial bottom line.

And finally, meet Nigel

Then we met Nigel, partner in a firm of angel investors[48] called Truestone. Nigel told me,

We are only interested in investing in HiH if there is a measurable spiritual or social impact as a consequence of the investment.

Nobody has said that to me before. It seemed like the perfect fit.

You see, in my humble opinion, what makes the HiH model different is this:

48 Angel investors are individuals who invest financially in entrepreneurial business ventures.

1. Most people who go into business are successful business people. Then, out of their success, they want to do some good, but their main focus is business.
2. There are some businesses that want to tick the CSR (Corporate Social Responsibility) box just to make themselves look good.
3. There are those people that want to do good and generally do so by starting charities. If they start a business, they tend to do it with a 'charity' mindset and probably, at best, bounce along or, more likely, fail.

In contrast, HiH started as a charity and then realized that commercial business also had a response to poverty. We started our commercial business because we wanted to make a difference in people's lives. You see, our motive is not no. 1 or no. 2; we firmly wear commercial hats, with a view to the business responding to poverty.

I didn't know Nigel very well, although I could see he clearly was not a normal institutional investor. He seemed keen to support the work of HiH. To be fair (maybe not by now, but at that time), everyone who invested in us had to know there was a risk that they may never see their money again. Not only because I told them that, up front, but because it was obvious. We had no security, no collateral, no track record, nothing really.

Nigel was prepared to make an investment, we sorted out some paperwork and the deal was done.

Grant, please be careful

I was invited to a group I am associated with in order to give an update on the progress of HiH. After the meeting, one of the members, Gerald, came and talked to me about the business and asked if there was anything I needed. Well the simple answer to that is generally,

Money.

So we discussed a structure for the investment and, if I remember correctly, it wasn't so dissimilar to my arrangement with Henry where the money was left in a carrier bag at Euston. So we concluded and as the funds were transferred his final comment on the deal was,

Grant, please be careful.

I wasn't sure if he was referring to my handling of his investment or just advising me generally for when I was crossing the road.

CONFESSIONS OF A PROPERTY INVESTOR

To understand all of this properly, there's something else you need to know.

It begins in the late 1980s, when Sue and I had been sensing a call to go to Bible College. We reasoned that if we went to the church and asked for them to support us to go to Bible College, they would probably say, *yes*. Whilst this seemed pretty logical to us, it was not a confirmation that this was God's plan for our lives. So to be sure of his confirmation we prayed that, rather than us approach the church, our church would approach us about it and offer to support us. We prayed in that vein for 2 years.

Then one night, a friend popped round; his name was Roy (in fact his name still *is* Roy). As Roy was leaving he said in passing,

Have you ever thought about going freelance as a QS?
Most people just say, *goodnight* when they leave, but I didn't particularly think there was anything that strange about his statement. We went to bed, and as I was lying in semi-slumber – that point between consciousness and sleep – it hit me.

Freelance!

I could earn more money as a freelance QS, and I could either work part time and study part time, or work hard for 2 years and save the required funds to go to Bible college full time.

Sue, that's it!!!!
To which Sue immediately said, zzzzzzzzzzzzzzzzzzzzzzzzzzzzzz

The next day we prayed as to whether this was the right route to go down. Now, the normal way people go freelance as a QS is they start to do some work for private clients and then, when they think they have enough work to make a living out of it, they quit their job. But not me: we wanted to know if this was God's purpose, and if so I would quit the job straight away and start freelancing.

I put out a couple of feelers, and one person, Ian, immediately said he would give me work. Over the next couple of weeks, I pushed to find out how much work and how serious he was. Ian then became evasive and non-committal. One night, Sue and I prayed,

If Ian Wilson doesn't commit tomorrow, then we will assume we are not to go freelance.

When I got into work the following day, there was a note on my desk, saying that Ian had called and wanted me to call him back.

I rang and he invited me over for supper that evening to discuss what I could do for him as a freelance surveyor. I went that evening, discussed the prospects, came home to Sue and told her of our conversation. We considered this to be the sign from God we had asked for, I handed in my notice and left a month later. Interestingly, Ian wasn't offering me enough work to live on, but that didn't actually matter. What was more significant to us was that God had responded and given us a sign, and we had confidence to move forward into freelance work, knowing the ultimate goal would be fulfilled.

Within 3 months, I gained 2 other clients and was earning triple what I had been earning in paid employment. Sue and I looked at this situation and concluded that the reason we went freelance was in response to God's guiding, so this triple income was really God's, not ours.

I then had another idea: if we invest this money properly, not only could we finance Bible college, we could also provide an income for the rest of our lives and I would never have to take on paid employment again and we could give all our time to 'ministry' (as we understood ministry in those days). So we began to pray about what we should invest in, and we came to the conclusion that property was the way to go. We prayed again and God led us to buy a property in Lanzarote in a complex with its own private pool (let's be honest, if you are going to buy property, Lanzarote is certainly the place to do it).

Then we prayed again and we were led to buy another house in the town in which we lived; I needed to refurbish it, and with this came a building plot where we could build another property. So God led us to having 3 potential rentable properties, in addition to the one we lived in. Everything was falling into place and God was providing for our finances in a way we never imagined.

Then ...

This was in the late 1980s; any of you as old as me may remember what happened next. We had made our purchases on borrowed money, based on financing the loans through rental incomes. Basically, as I remember it, overnight interest rates trebled and property prices fell through the floor. Good job God led us to buy in Lanzarote then, because obviously that won't be affected by the collapse in the UK ... except that it was UK buyers that were pushing the prices up in Lanzarote and we had borrowed in the UK for the Spanish property.

Then ...

The swimming pool in our private complex sprung a leak and a dispute arose between the owners of the private complex over who should pay for the repairs. The result was that we had a property in Lanzarote, with a rising monthly mortgage cost in a complex with its own private 'hole'. Who do you think wanted to go there? In fact, as the UK economy wobbled, who would have had the desire to go there, even if our private 'hole' was full of chlorinated water? The house we were going to refurbish was still being refurbished, and few people like renting a house from you whilst you're still injecting a new DPC (damp-proof course). The plot clearly had no house on it and it's difficult to rent a house which isn't built. So income was approximately £0 and expenditure was approximately 'very high'.

So, our situation had altered slightly from how we had envisaged it. Apparently, if you put a frog in boiling water (don't try this at home) it will jump out. But if you put a frog in a pan of cold water and slowly heat the water (don't try this at home either) you will slowly boil the frog.

In February 1992, I was in Boston in Lincolnshire. I was now working about 60 or 70 hours a week just to keep all our loans going, we had sold the CAT, rented out the lawn mower and bought woolly jumpers to save on central heating. I was driving back from Boston at 9pm and, believe it or not, came to the conclusion:

This has all gone very wrong!

I came home to Sue that night and had formulated a prayer. I ran the prayer by Sue, because I didn't want God hearing it if Sue didn't agree. With Sue's approval, we then presented our prayer to God, although I guess God had already heard it:

God, this has gone very wrong. We were going to go to Bible college in September 1993; right now that is completely financially ridiculous, but if that is what you want for us, you can make it happen. If we do not go to Bible college in September 1993, we will take it that you do not want us to go and we will never mention the subject of Bible college again.

We went to bed satisfied that we had plotted the way ahead, relying on God for the future. We also told nobody else about our prayer. A few months later, I was travelling round the M25 with Robert at 6.30am. Robert owned his own construction company and I was doing some freelance work for him, which was why we were driving round the M25 at 6.30am. Robert said to me,

Rachel and I have been praying about you and Sue. We know you would like to go to Bible college. If you were prepared to carry on doing some work for me, we would pay you what you need to live on to be able to go and study.

My immediate response? Well, I laughed.

Robert didn't understand my laughter, so I told him,

You have no idea what we need to live on, we are effectively financing 4 properties and have no rental income.

Robert's response?

No, you didn't listen: I said Rachel and I have prayed about this and this was what God told us to do.

I stopped laughing.

∿∿∿∿∿∿∿∿∿∿∿∿∿∿∿∿∿∿∿∿∿∿∿∿∿∿

It's too late to write, 'To cut a long story short…', but to cut an even longer story a little bit shorter, we went to Bible college in September 1993. The property was sold in Lanzarote at a significant loss, the plot of land was sold, the refurbishment was concluded and the house was rented out. The experience in interest payments and lost capital value cost us around £100k. Even as I write this, it turns my stomach because of the hard work and effort which concluded with pouring that £100k down the drain. It was such a waste, but we did fulfil the original purpose of going to Bible college.

So what do you learn through all that? How does that shape the future?

Well firstly, every step we took we believed God directed us, but did he? Because at one level it was a massive time-consuming, energy-sapping mistake. Did we learn through it? Can we claim that 'God works for good'[49] (in all circumstances) and that God was there? Well, we lived to tell the story, and we went to Bible college.

But instead of praying, what if we had gone to a financial advisor?

Certainly the consequence of this experience has made us more conservative in our actions than some might be.

But maybe most importantly, and many will think most disappointingly, never again have I said,

God has told me to …

I admire those that do, I don't laugh at them and say,

You don't have a clue what you are talking about, because actually God doesn't work like that.

That would be bang out of order, because I believe God can guide like that. But I still find it hard to summon the confidence in myself to interpret his guidance for the future. What I do say, with hindsight, is that I can see how God has led us. But my confidence in saying,

49 Romans 8:28.

God has said … has gone.

I am sure as you read these words, some of you will feel a little sad; some of you will think,

Get over yourself.

And some of you will say,

We're not surprised, God doesn't speak like that today.

My faith and trust in God haven't changed; I certainly don't blame God for my stomach turning when I think about the lost £100k. You can argue with me that God was with us right the way through, and that as a consequence of the experience Sue and I are closer to God. I wouldn't strongly disagree with that, but I would argue that if I was a different person, less stubborn and probably less arrogant, I could have learnt what we learnt a bit quicker rather than it taking 5 years out of our lives.

Christian faith is a journey, and, hopefully, along that journey we learn. If you stick your head above the parapet, you are vulnerable. But don't ever conclude that God can't be trusted. God can always be trusted. The challenge is understanding what he is doing with us.

Maybe one thing I should add is that I worked with Robert for about 25 years, and we are still strong friends with him and his wife, Rachel. I worked with Ian Wilson for a similar amount of time, about 25 years, and he and the family also became great friends.

And why have I told this story here? Because it is important to understand that we haven't got it right all the time – although, to be fair, you had probably worked that out already. It is important to understand that there is no simple formula to business that works all the time.

My concept of buying property and renting, in a different economic climate, could have worked, but for me it was the wrong time in the wrong place. But the most important point is the conclusion of the story: I didn't limp away, lick my wounds and go back to freelance surveying. God took us to Bible college in a miraculous way, and we came out having learnt a life lesson, feeling blessed by friends who God worked through and eagerly looking for 'what next.'

Interlude over, back to the main event.

The conclusion I come to is that this has all been in God's hands. If you read the stories above, one is incredible, two are amazing; but the stories just go on and on. Small sums of money to start with, which slowly get larger and larger. Today we are discussing investment from pension funds; those don't get out of bed for under £50m! We are talking to high-net-worth individuals who are professional investors with large amounts to commit. What is interesting is that you then gain traction; once you say a pension fund is in talks about investing, that gives HiH a credibility that shows we are worth investing in. I believe that God has crossed our path with investors at the right time of our growth curve. As for the investors, somehow God prepared them so that they were excited by the prospect of what HiH could do with their investment. I really can't explain it any more than that, because there is no logical sense to why such investment came when it did.

In recent years, there has being a growing awareness of 'impact investment'. Impact investment makes a strong financial return, but also has some form of community, social or spiritual impact. It has opened up opportunities for both investors and businesses to think about business in a different way. This isn't unique to HiH, but certainly it would seem to be a case of 'right place, right time'!

POINTS TO PONDER

- You never know who you might be sitting next to.
- It doesn't matter what time breakfast is served, if you have been invited – go.
- If you are looking for investment, look in the bins at Euston Station.
- Always trust that God knows what he is doing.

CHAPTER 12

LET'S BUILD

Right place, right time. We all know what we mean by this.

I was travelling with an acquaintance from Iringa to Arusha in Tanzania. To achieve this journey by bus, you change at 'Junction' – a lorry stop. My travelling partner and I arrived at Junction at 3pm. The last bus of the day left for Arusha at 1pm. My travelling partner suggested that we pray, which is never a bad idea. After a fair time praying, I ask,

What are you praying for?

A bus, was his reply.

I like to think I'm a man of some faith, but even I knew that wasn't the right prayer. The last bus left at 1pm, and for all I appreciate that God is outside of time, we're not. The point being: you can be in the wrong place at the right time, and in the right place at the wrong time, either is likely to end in disappointment.

WHAT'S PRAYER ALL ABOUT?

Let me explain my understanding of prayer here. To me, prayer isn't just a spiritual transaction of 'I want something, so I will pray I get it.' Prayer isn't just about wanting something, and praying for it. Often our prayer is well-intentioned, our motives are good, but we completely miss the point. Let me a give an example: my friend has cancer, so I pray for her healing. But wait, God is the creator of my friend and I believe God can heal cancer. So if God is creator and God can heal cancer, then why did my friend get cancer in the first place? And why does she still have it? To me, if we are to understand anything from the book of Job, it isn't *all* about the healing; it is about the journey with God for both my friend with cancer and me as her praying friend. It is about recognizing our need for God and journeying closer to him in our need. I am of the belief that prayer is not about the outcome, but more to do with the journey.

Therefore, I don't generally pray for buses or even cancer,[50] I pray for what God wants to teach me or my friends next, so that I am closer to God tomorrow.

That might suggest I don't believe in prayer, but I believe in 1 Thessalonians 5:17[51] as much as anyone. Because by constantly praying, God is shaping our understanding, making us into the person he wants us to be. As we then move into that way of thinking, it actually means I don't have to pray about every decision in the day because my

50 Which is my personal approach to prayer, and while undoubtedly imperfect, it is influenced, among other things, by losing that £100k.

51 Pray continually.

understanding of God has a godly default position. To give an extreme example, if I am invited to a strip club, I don't have to pray about whether to go or not; my journey with God tells me that is not a helpful place to go. That, as I say, is extreme, but there are many other decisions I am able to make without specifically praying for them, because I understand God's best for my life.

I fear that, at times, we don't analyse the responses we do or don't get from God in our prayers. So sometimes, it appears that God answers, i.e. we get what we want; and sometimes it appears that he doesn't, i.e. we don't get what we want. If we don't reflect on how God responds to our prayers, we could come to the conclusion that this prayer thing is a bit of a lottery. That is why I said that, whilst we prayed about going to Bible college, and whilst we *thought* we had God's clear guidance, on reflection did God actually confirm our direction? Or did we manipulate the answers into what we wanted to hear? And that is why now, if I'm truly honest, I am less sure, I have less confidence, and am no longer able to boldly stand and say,

> *This is the word of the Lord, I am to go and build a 10-storey office block for every charity in Nairobi.*

But I am very comfortable about saying,

> *Look at what the Lord has done – a 10-storey office block, with apprenticeships and income to become self-sustaining, for CMS Africa in Nairobi.*

So perhaps, as we waited at the lorry stop, our prayer should have been,

> *Lord, what do we do now?*

or,

> Lord, give us the patience to handle the next 12 hours in this godforsaken outpost,

or,

> What is the reason we missed that bus, is there something you want us to do here at the lorry stop?

And the answer might be,

> You timed your journey badly, go and find somewhere to sleep and I'll see you in the morning.

BACK TO THE (CONSTRUCTION) PLOT ...

Construction in Kenya now is the right place, and the right time, with Kenya experiencing economic growth. One consequence is a growing middle class, and, with that, a demand for houses. The actual demand for new houses currently is 150,000 per year, every year. There are only about 35,000 being built. As I said, construction in Kenya is ... right place, right time.

That doesn't mean there aren't difficulties.

For our first construction project, we formed a company, Hand in Hand Development Ltd, which was managed by Joshua[52] and myself. In turn, we formed a Joint Venture partnership with another Kenyan company. As a UK board, we discussed this project, deliberating as to whether we should get involved. Our conclusion was that we wouldn't meet all our goals, but it would put us on the map to be recognized as being able to manage big projects.

That first JV construction project took around 2 years to procure: purchasing 23 acres of potential development

---

52 Joshua the husband of Gladys, the same Joshua we met back in Chapter 5.

land; financing this initial stage 50:50; refining the design; considering all our options; eventually going to tender; narrowing our discussion down to 3 potential contractors; deciding who we want to go with; final negotiations ... then we start!

As we procured the project and we came up with designs, we always asked ourselves the question,

Would we live there?

If the answer was *no*, we went back to the drawing board. For example, we wanted to create a secure environment, but I had also been to housing projects where there were 7ft high walls around every compound, giving a very harsh feel to the environment. We therefore wanted to make the whole compound secure for the 200 houses, but allow that each individual compound was surrounded by plant life and chain link. This gave a very open feel to the estate, making it feel spacious and more of a community, and less of a concrete jungle where nobody talks to each other.

The very first activity the contractor undertook was to deliver a lorry load of timber to site. This was a momentous occasion; I was emailed a photo of the lorry, the timber and the site. Possibly, right place, right time?

I rang one of our investors and shared our moment of excitement, anticipation and realization that, after 2 years of preparation, we finally had 'broken ground' or, put another way, had a lorry load of timber delivered.

This took place during September and October, which is the rainy season in Kenya. Nairobi had been experiencing a particularly wet period that year. The day after the delivery of timber, we learnt that our chosen contractor, who was involved in other projects in Nairobi, had had so much rain on another project that the building he was working on had collapsed. We were consequently informed that the contractor would be withdrawing from our project. In fact, he was withdrawing from everything. In actual fact, to this day he has never been seen in Kenya again.

24 hours after my previous call to our investor, I had to make a 2nd call:

You know we started yesterday? Today we stopped!

And the response,

We could have gone to Kenya, built 1 house, employed a few people, made profit and everyone would have seen that as a success and then we would have moved on to the next project.

We could have gone to Kenya, built 10 houses, employed a few people, made a profit and everyone would have seen that as a success, and then we would have moved on to the next project.

But no, you went to Kenya and decided to build 200 houses, what did you expect?

On this project, after the initial equity investment, we arranged bank finance to complete phase 1. This was uncharted territory for me, and took so long that we basically ran out of cash for several weeks whilst the bank crossed every 't' and dotted every 'i'. There was one stage where it seemed unbelievable, as if having got everything agreed and having put my granny up for security, there was still something I hadn't done right. I was assured by my fellow directors this was not the case, it was just the tortoise-like nature of all banks.

As a consequence of cash flow issues we have sometimes progressed with a bit of a limp in our step, or a stone in our shoe, or a thorn in our side or 3 wheels on our wagon. And so, as a management board, much of our discussion has been around sales and speed of construction. In some board meetings people have become quite excitable. At the end of one such meeting, one director concluded that the debate which had taken place was healthy, because if we all thought the same, there would be no point in having 4 board members. I do think that is a very important point, as long as you can have 'excitable' debate and retain respect for one another.

As a JV board, it was decided that we needed to have a retreat to reflect on what had gone well, what needed improving and what needed changing altogether. As we discussed all this, we came to the conclusion that we were working well as a JV but HiH needed to have more 'hands on' involvement. It was suggested that HiH should be given the opportunity to build 24 houses ourselves.

You see, up until now, HiH had been involved in procurement and my input had been as a QS, but HiH being responsible for the build itself was a new venture, which I didn't know if we were up to.

As we sat around the table, Joshua immediately responded,

Thanks for this opportunity, when do we start?

My instant reaction? That's all very well, but this is a big jump for HiH. However, after thinking it through a little more, I came to the conclusion that I agreed with Joshua, it just took me a little longer to work it through. To date, due to switching demands (improved road networks elsewhere in Nairobi), we still actually haven't built the 24 houses, but I am sure the day is coming.

~~~~~~~~~~~~~~~~~~~~~~~~~~~~~

Obviously one way to get money into the company is to sell houses. As well as the marketing team, the directors were doing what they could to find buyers. Alongside our business activities, Hand in Hand Charity had decided to register a sister charity in Kenya, which became the Hand in Hand Foundation. Someone had recommended I go and see a man called Isaac who could register Hand in Hand Foundation for us there. I went to Isaac's office, bearing in mind we haven't met before, we commenced with polite conversation, me talking about other Kenyans I know, etc., etc.

Isaac then asks: *What else do you do in Kenya?*
Me: *We are building houses.*
Isaac: *Do you have any information?*
I hand Isaac a brochure.
Isaac: *How much are these selling for?*
I state the price.
Isaac: *I'll buy one.*
I laugh.
Isaac: *Why are you laughing?*
Me: *Well, I walked into your office 30 minutes ago, before which you didn't know me from Adam, you haven't seen the houses and you haven't discussed this with your wife.*
Isaac: *From the people you have told me you know and*

your relationships, you are obviously a man of God. If you have lied to me, that is your problem. I have been impressed by your story and I want to buy one.

When something sounds too good to be true it normally is, but not this time! Isaac obviously didn't buy 1 house … he bought 2! I still don't know if he has been to see them or told his wife!

And on reflection, there is no question that our relationship with the JV has taken us into a level of construction that has been a challenge. Probably the most significant outcome is that we both know we are trustworthy partners and share similar commitments to the product we are creating.

Our main achievement in building these houses was that we did produce a quality product, and generally people were very happy with the standard of finish. As for the *'would we be happy to live there?'* test: I bought a house myself, more to put finance into the project than anything, and yes, I would have been very happy to live there. We did make sure our workers were protected, insisting on boots, helmets and hi-vis jackets. Did we pay above the minimum wage? To be honest, I don't know. I think so, but I can't really know, as we employed a Kenyan contractor and only he can tell the truth in that regard. And finally, with experience under our belts, we have now moved on to other construction projects.

The downside was that the project took far too long. The cost of financing was significant and although everyone thinks development projects are a license to print money, we actually didn't make money selling houses; where our profit has come from is the growth in land value. With hindsight, it would have been more profitable to buy 23 acres, watch it grow in value and sell it, but holding land doesn't create jobs. The project didn't fully achieve our social ambitions: yes, we looked after some people's medical needs; yes, we gave a Christmas bonus; yes, we completed a quality product; but in my view, as previously predicted, it didn't really achieve HiH goals and it took a long time not to achieve them.

However, also as previously predicted, what it did do was put us on the map as being able to undertake significant construction projects. Many know about HiH's involvement in the project, although to be fair they probably don't know the extent of our involvement.

THE NEXT STEP

One day, on my way back to the airport, I receive a phone call from Jane. Jane asks if I have time for a cup of tea, I do and so we meet. She represents a Christian organization that owns a plot of land in Westlands. Westlands is the Kensington of Nairobi. The charity had purchased the land about 50 years ago, when it was worth a few thousand pounds. Today, as Nairobi has grown, it is now a prime location, literally worth millions of sterling and ripe for office development. They had found a developer to build on their plot. The developer had carried out a feasibility study and concluded that they could finance a 10-storey office block, charge 45% Project Management fees and, for the privilege, they would keep the rental income for 25 years.

After this, the building would become owned 100% by the charity. Jane was acting as the lawyer for the charity and concluded that the above arrangement was possibly taking advantage, and she wanted to know if HiH could offer a more beneficial structure.

The problem you have here is that charities have no money to build 10-storey office blocks, because they spend all their money on the work of the charity. They also generally know little about building 10-storey office blocks, so they go to people who do know. Unfortunately, people who build 10-storey office blocks generally know that charities know little about building 10-storey office blocks. So what happens is that charities slowly come to the conclusion that there is a pond out there full of developers swimming around looking for projects, but so many of these developers are sharks ready to bite your left leg off and when there is nothing left of the left leg, they come back for the right!

Without even looking at the development plan, I knew we could offer a better deal that both benefitted the charity and fulfilled the aims of HiH. This is where Briken EA Ltd began: Terry and HiH formed a development management company, with a particular focus on developing other Christian charities' land in the city, structuring a relationship between the charity and ourselves which is mutually beneficial. Let me stress here, HiH is a commercial company, and we finance commercially. Our skill is our ability to create a relationship which prevents the charity losing both its legs to sharks!

Our model was very simple. Terry and I discussed the challenge of various methods of financing. It was Terry who came up with the idea of an equity share for the landowner equivalent to the land value. Terry and I then went to meet the charity and we explained the concept, which even I understood. The charity can't believe the impact of our proposal, we shake hands and get into the car to leave. At this point Terry looks at me and says,

So where are you going to get the money from?

Me: *Well, it was your idea, I thought you knew where to get the money from!!*

So having got a great concept we now had no idea where to get the money. The difficulty for the land owner in Kenya is: if they go to the banks, will the banks be prepared to lend? But overcoming that hurdle, which is a significant one, if the banks are prepared to lend, they will require the first 20% to be put in by the land owner – in this case $1.6m. Obviously, CMS Africa (the African branch of Christian Mission Society) do not have $1.6m; all the funds that come in are spent on their mission. So unless you have a developer who becomes the missional partner, who is looking out for the best for the mission, these organizations are either strangled by the banks or taken advantage of by developers who know the land owner has few choices.

Around this time, Terry's church was holding a conference with a speaker from the UK. Terry calls me and asks if I know of the speaker, because he manages an impact investment fund. It turns out that the speaker has offices in London and I go to meet him. After a couple of meetings, I am asked two questions,

How much has Terry put in financially in your businesses?
How much have you put in financially?

I respond to the first question. The second question is a little harder. You see, Sue and I have never had money, I am not saying we are poor, but even when you look at how we lost £100k, that wasn't money we had sitting in the bank and lost through unwise investment, it was money earned through my surveying activities and immediately spent on servicing loans – money which was never recovered. We have generally worked on the principle that we will earn what we would like to live on, but we have never had capital in the bank, because instead of earning more money, we have invested our time into HiH. So the answer to the question is, *nothing*. At this point the speaker, who is sitting on a wheely chair, pushes his chair back across the floor and says,

I have never heard that before, so you have basically leveraged your reputation to encourage people to invest?

I had never looked at it quite like that before, but I guess so! And from there, the due diligence process began.

CMS AFRICA

Sometime later, we were pursuing the development of another Nairobi plot which was becoming impossible, due to various obstacles. However, we now had investment, and therefore found ourselves in the ridiculous position of having immediate access to finance, but potentially nothing to spend it on. It has to be said, it was a rather unusual position with which I was heretofore unfamiliar. As we were chewing this over in our UK office, Emma, my PA, said,

Why don't you call Dennis?

I said,

Dennis has funding, he has no need for us and I don't want to confuse his current relationships.

Emma said,

Ring him.

Over the course of my life, I have had many meetings with people – people I have been introduced to or advised to meet – and the relationship goes nowhere. There have been meetings with some people about whom, after the first encounter, I have thought that the relationship would take us places, but to date it hasn't. Then there are people who I have met who end up becoming a significant part of my life. Like Dennis.

I was first introduced to Revd Dr Dennis Tongoi in 2012. At that time, he was CEO of CMS Africa. Dennis speaks very fast, possibly because he has so much going through his head that he has to get it out fast, either before he forgets it, or in order to cover as much ground as possible. I have always perceived CMS UK as being a relatively traditional missional organization. Speaking to Dennis, I very quickly realized that CMS Africa had a completely different approach to mission, training and enabling business being one of their main foci – enabling people to find faith and yet sustaining them physically.

CMS Africa occupied 0.6 of an acre in a prime area of Nairobi. The land had been given to CMS Africa in 2003, when CMS UK purchased the land for the sum of $23k and gifted it to CMS Africa. As already described, with the growth of the Kenyan economy and the expansion of Nairobi, the piece of land was now worth $1.7m. When I met Dennis, he had a vision to build a 16-storey office block, 6 floors of parking and 10 floors of office space. Dennis seemed to have many finance options available to him for the development, so I wished him well and we parted company.

So, when Emma said I should ring him, being the obedient person I am, I called. Dennis' response was for us to meet when I was next in Nairobi. Continuing in my obedience, I met with Dennis. Dennis explained that the consultants had been working on the procurement for some time, and the building design was complete, but there was actually no confirmed current funding. My response to Dennis was that we potentially had a funding partner, but there was one non-negotiable for us to enter a working relationship: that CMS Africa would have to change their quantity surveyor to Fanisi Consultants, as we had worked with them for 10 years and had a strong relationship, and wouldn't trust the management of finance to any other consultant. Dennis immediately responded saying,

That won't cause a problem, Fanisi are the QS already on the team.

So we embarked on the project, refining the current design a little, going to tender and appointing a contractor. The works commenced on 1 August 2016. Almost as soon as the basement was excavated, I witnessed rain in Nairobi like I couldn't remember; the basement turned into a very large, dirty swimming pool. On one occasion even the excavators were fully immersed in the water. Twice the project was stopped by officials, twice the construction team were sent home, twice the said bodies were looking for their 'facilitation', twice we responded to their spurious demands and twice we did not 'facilitate' and the site went back to work.

The construction was finished on time and under budget. Both of those are relatively unheard of around the world, let alone in Kenya. To achieve both can only be due to an extremely efficient project team or a miracle, and my money would be on both.

Here are the outcomes:

- 150 construction workers employed for 18 months and paid above the minimum wage. If each construction worker is responsible for just 5 people, that is 750 adults and children supported, with no donor support, purely through the hard work of their relative or spouse.
- 16 apprenticeships facilitated by the contractor in order to bring to life the classroom teaching at their training school and prepare those students to be employment ready.
- Returns achieved for the investors who took the risk to invest in Africa.
- Beautiful, modern offices for the activities of CMS Africa, in the hub of Nairobi.
- As a consequence of CMS Africa's equity share, the potential annual rental income of the space which is CMS Africa's share is in the region of $200k. That's

this year and every year. This is income which will support the work of CMS Africa, and assist in growing their programmes with certain income, which is not dependent on donor goodwill or generosity. It is commercial, inflation-proofed income, which belongs 100% to CMS Africa, with no influence from some well-meaning, but ill-informed donor who has a particular leaning to producing leather placemats and who caveats their giving with such conditions.

- Due to the enterprising acumen of Dennis, who has continued to negotiate with banks and financers, he could purchase 2 additional floors. The intention is for CMS Africa to purchase these floors from Dennis at some point in the future, which will create a further rental income in the region of $200k.

- CMS Africa retain the head lease, so when other current buyers of office space decide at some point in the future to move to other premises, CMS Africa have the first opportunity to buy those offices, which has the potential to generate a further $600k annual income.

- The resulting maximum benefit could be an additional $1m annual income to CMS Africa. Their previous income was $400k, of which about $300k was contributed by CMS UK. The outstanding $100k was generated through fundraising, or rather product from business activities. As a result of Dennis' trust in God, innovation and tenacity, CMS Africa could triple their income, which will triple their programmes, which will triple their impact, and all with Kenyan income.

Now that is what I call impact investing.

That was the start of a relationship whereby Briken EA Ltd would find and manage development projects on prime land owned by Christians, and an introduction to investors who would finance the development. We have actually had investors approach us with comments like,

If we were to invest in Kenya, we would really like to do it through you guys, seeing as you have your feet on the ground.

And as I related this story to a friend of mine, his response was,

Who else could turn a brush salesman/used-petrol-pump dealer into an international property developer?

POINTS TO PONDER

- Where there's a will there's a way.
- There is no challenge that we can't handle with God on our side.
- Reputation isn't just who you are, it's who your friends are too.
- Don't wait for a bus after 1pm at 'Junction'; it's not coming.

CHAPTER 13

SO WHERE NEXT?

SHALL WE BUY LAND?

Buying land in Africa is fraught with challenge. Not least is the question of whether you are actually buying from the registered owner. There are too many stories of land purchase nightmares. One particular landowner witnessed a developer building houses on his land: another party, who wasn't actually the owner, had supposedly sold the land to the developer. So the real owner simply watched the construction grow, and once it was complete he went to the developer, took possession of the construction and thanked him for developing his land for him. There are many stories like this. For this reason, you often see signs saying,

This plot is not for sale.

So if you see a sign saying,

This plot is not for sale,

you can be pretty confident that whoever is trying to sell it to you doesn't actually own it.

Hand in Hand work with a lawyer who is completely trustworthy and who has kept us from falling into false agreements. But buying land is a time-consuming business, with researching land titles and other challenges, in fact anything else you haven't already thought of. One plot we were buying got caught up in a caveat. Basically, in layman's language, the agreement was suspended, which you may notice is not the same as cancelled. If I understand it correctly, a caveat works something like this:

I agree to buy a house from you; we agree the price and I pay you the money. Your next door neighbour puts a caveat on the sale, saying that her dog has always played in your garden and therefore has 'animal rights' to access. You, the landowner, then have to prove that the dog doesn't have such rights. In the meantime, neither of us can withdraw from the sale, because we have signed the agreement. So we are both jammed.

In this case, we had paid the money for the land and a caveat was raised. Everybody involved felt comfortable the problem would get solved quickly; we even had a letter on file stating that the lawyer anticipated this would be concluded within a month of the caveat being filed. Two and a half years later, the case has just now been settled. Now, in this particular case, the land has appreciated significantly in that time, outweighing our costs – i.e. the cost of finance – but the story could have been quite different.

SO WHERE NEXT?

I was with another investor in Kenya one day, let's call them 'Jelly Fish'. Jelly Fish asks,

How can we provide quality housing which has an asset value for the 60% of Kenyans that live on £1.50 a day?

My response,

I don't know.

And Jelly Fish says,

That's what every developer says, because actually most developers don't have the will to find the solution. But I actually think HiH do have a will to find a solution, because you want to see 60% of Kenyans lifted out of poverty. If we could find a way to house them with a property that has value and that they own, this would contribute to doing just that.

That night I lie awake in bed with my head spinning. Why is my head spinning? I am trying to work out:

1. How do we find a solution to creating a house which has value for a person living on £1.50 a day?
2. But, and possibly more significantly, why has nobody got an answer? Is Jelly Fish right: the reason there is no answer is because there is no will to find an answer?
3. And, if we don't find an answer, are we the same as everybody else?

With this spinning around in my head, and the reality dawning on me that sleep is not going to happen anytime soon, I get a text message. Normally, when I get texts at midnight in Kenya it is somebody from the UK who is either unaware I am in Kenya, or unaware of the time difference. Like the time my son Joe rang at 11.30pm. Joe never rings when I am in the UK, let alone when I am in Kenya. So I take his call thinking it must be serious, only for him to ask what the rice to water ratio for jambalaya is! Well, at least he thought I would know.

Actually the text message wasn't from the UK; it was from Terry. I tell him I am struggling to sleep because of the meeting. He tells me:

I am sure you will find an answer.

That's it, I have to get up. To which Sue responds,

And do you really think you are going to find an answer to this question in the next two hours?

~~~~~~~~~~~~~~~~~~~~~~~~~~~~~~~~~~~

The conclusion I come to is this: you build the smallest unit possible; around 15m^2 with shared washrooms and kitchen facilities. A 15m^2 unit can be built in Kenya for under £3,000, so let's give it a value of £4,000. In 4 years' time, that 15m^2 unit will be worth double. But a person, let's call him Bob, living on £1.50 per day, can't get a mortgage. Bob is currently paying between £10 and £15 a month for rent.

So here is the solution: you create a housing association (HA), which rents the houses out at £12 per month to Bob. As the unit grows in value, the HA shares that increase with

Bob. Let's say the HA awards Bob half the growth in value. This requires imaginative financing, but is based on the future growth in value of the smallest unit. Effectively, you are creating a let-to-buy scheme – nothing very imaginative about that!

In the same development, the HA builds a whole range of units, so there is always a bigger unit for Bob to aspire to and for Bob to trade up to (he can use the growth in value of any sized unit as a deposit to trade up to the next sized unit). After a period of time, with inflationary growth, even the poorest of people will own an asset value.

In Kenya, there are Circles. A Circle is a group of people who have organized to contribute something small to achieve something big. The HA could create a Circle, encouraging people to save 50p per day. After 5 years, each individual will have saved £750, or a couple will have saved £1,500; at today's prices that's 20%–40% of the selling price of the smallest unit. That could be used as a deposit, and the financer comes in with 60%–80% of the outstanding finance.

What is important is that this is a commercial arrangement, which is dependent on imaginative finance. There are actually groups who possibly would be prepared to donate large amounts of money to finance the other 60%–80%. This is OK, but that money will run out. If the 60%–80% is financed by investors, who are either getting a smaller return or having to wait longer for their return, more money will be available. It won't run out, and the poorest are housed commercially rather than through donations. Not only that, but if the Circle concept works, the HA are creating a far higher level of ownership, and are also marketing their venture.

In my view, the current slums will never really be replaced. They are communities, vibrant economies all of their own, and it would be wrong – an affront to the occupiers – to remove their homes and livelihood without consultation. But an affordable housing association scheme would create a choice – an attractive alternative, a safe environment – within a managed development, and, most importantly, it would represent an asset value for the poorest households.

So, Jelly Fish, there's the solution. I don't dispute it needs refining, it needs a lot of hard work, a lot of community and trust will need to be created, and an acknowledgement that not every development will work. Therefore, now it is back to the Jelly Fishes of this world who really want to make an impact investment.

If you are reading this (which obviously you are) and you don't think my model will work, then you now have the same challenge as I have. Don't just dismiss my model, make it better, make it stronger, make it work, either with Hand in Hand, or some other organization; but if you just dismiss the idea and give no alternative, then how clever are you?

MY BIBLICAL REFLECTION

Let's take the story of the *minas* in Luke 19[53] and apply it to my situation. I have been given a *mina*[54] in the form of my skill as a quantity surveyor, and with that skill I have 3 options:

53 Luke 19:10–26.
54 A *mina* was a sum of money, equivalent to about 3 months' wages.

1. Reject quantity surveying as a capitalist tool and bury it.
2. Make a comfortable living for my family, try to be a good witness through my surveying career, and give 10% back to God.
3. Go to Kenya, find the finance to build 5,000,000 affordable houses, create an asset and a decent home for people, and repay the money to the investor.

Those are the choices I have to make as the person God has made me. Or perhaps we go to Matthew 25 and the parable of the talents.[55] I would consider that I have been given 5 talents and that there is an expectation of me to deliver. If I go for option 1 above, that would be me acting like the 3rd servant who the master describes as a 'wicked, lazy servant'. If I go for option 2, that is possibly acceptable, but if I go for option 3, I will have been up for the task God has equipped me for and gone for it to demonstrate the sovereignty of God in my life. Of course, before I get complacent, there could be an option 4:

Go into all the world and build low cost housing!
And that brings me back down to earth!

~~~~~~~~~~~~~~~~~~~~~~~~~~~~

I am still kept awake at night sometimes, not because of worrying about tomorrow, but because we haven't implemented a solution to the housing challenge of those living on less than £1.50 per day. But there is a solution

---

55 Matthew 25: 14–29.

out there, and I may well have that solution, or you may well have it. And please introduce yourself to HiHG if you have a genuine low-cost solution. As I was literally putting the finishing touches to this book, I was introduced to a company (let's call them 'Make it Happen'), that are involved in system-build[56] house construction in Kenya. The supposed advantage of system-build houses is that they are cheaper and quicker to build. However, in my experience what so often happens in reality is that the group who have come up with the system-build design although they will make the end product slightly cheaper than traditional construction, they tend to benefit more themselves, rather than passing the saving on. But the company I met with not only seemed genuine in the desire to construct houses at the lowest possible rate, but they also manufacture their own panels, which cuts out the profit of the manufacturer. I'm a QS, so I count things; let me explain what I am getting at:

Traditional build
- Costs to build (in Kenya) £200/m^2
- Sells at £300/m^2
- Profit to the contractor £100/m^2 (50%)

Typical system-build
- Costs to build (in Kenya) £80/m^2
- Sells at £250/m^2
- Profit to system-build contractor £170/m^2 (213%)
- Saving to buyer £50/m^2 (20%)

56 Building with prefabricated components to speed up building construction.

Make it Happen
- Costs to build (in Kenya) £80/m^2
- Sells at £120/m^2
- Profit to 'Make it Happen' £40/m^2 (50%)
- Saving to the buyer £180/m^2 (250%)

These are approximate numbers, and of course being a numbers person, there are a few ways of calculating the percentages. That said, in this meeting I realized that at last, I'd come across a company that is serious about making a housing asset more affordable. Again, if you have just read this and I have annoyed you, get in touch, because I am happy to be proved wrong.

Then in the same week, I have been introduced to a man who is working on affordable housing for a charity I really respect, in partnership with Department for International Development (DfID) in another part of Africa. Now I think maybe there is a potential relationship here between 'Make it Happen', DfID and this man on achieving the best possible outcome for those that can't afford proper housing.

And so what still keeps me awake? Possibly it's that there must be an answer to this challenge, but whilst we keep looking for the answer, and as we search for like-minded people who genuinely want to make a difference in people's lives, David is still not getting paid enough to feed his family, grandmothers are living in tin sheds struggling to feed their grandchildren, and I know I am not doing:

Everything we can.

The moral of this chapter is: I was quite happy as a surveyor in the UK. I was making money to provide for my family, I enjoyed what I did, I was successful at what I did and there was little risk attached. I could have carried on doing it. But by starting HiHG, the potential social and spiritual returns are so much greater than staying in my own backyard. That to me is the challenge: God hadn't asked me to become a marine biologist, he asked me to do what I am good at and use it for a bigger end game. I could have said *no*, but who would have missed out?

And what is our business model? When I coat a brick in cement, and then another, and stick them together, value is created. Every time. Most times that value belongs to the investor or the one who can afford to finance the investment. Our model, building on land belonging to Christians, or creating a Housing Association, is to work with the investor to share the growth in value with those that are usually excluded from the growth in value.

SO HOW DID WE GET HERE?

I talked to a Kenyan with an idea at a conference, let's call him Peter. Peter suggests I talk to Gladys, Gladys talks with her husband and says,

When Grant gets involved things happen.

Joshua asks if I would like to do real estate in Kenya. We build houses, which don't meet our end game objectives.

But then, HiH get invited to partner with Christian

charities, realize their land value, create training and ultimately create fairly-paid employment.

If at first you can't achieve everything you want to, do it anyway, as long as it is not moving you in the opposite direction. It is far easier to steer a moving ship than to start it moving from the docks. Given the opportunity to do something which doesn't fulfil your ambition, do it. Some may criticize; ignore them, as long as you know where you are heading. But keep yourself accountable to a board or a mentor, just in case you enjoy the other road too much.

POINTS TO PONDER

- If you see a sign saying, *This land is not for sale*, do not try to buy it.
- If you are a light sleeper, don't think about the problems of low-cost housing before bed.
- If you haven't found the answer, keep looking.

CHAPTER 14

GOD CAN BE TRUSTED (BUT HE DOESN'T HALF MAKE IT HARD AT TIMES)

I once had a personal trainer for a few weeks. The reason? I wanted to lose 6kg. Ever since I was a child, I have had what I would call a 'rotund' body shape. It's not that I am particularly large, but I am not particularly 'sharp' either. As you get older, the right balance becomes harder and harder to achieve. So I hired a PT for 6 weeks to see if I could achieve that 6kg goal. It was one of the worst decisions I ever made. I came to dread the sessions: I was convinced that she was pushing me just to the point where you would need to call an ambulance, but knew exactly where to stop, which was perhaps the only reassuring aspect of the session. I had only paid for an hour and I definitely wasn't going into extra time. All the way through the session I would glance at the clock; only 58 minutes to go, I won't let her get the better of me, I don't quit and I am not quitting now. Every session ended the same way: completely exhausted, gasping for breath and waving goodbye to my PT because I couldn't speak.

Despite my lack of appetite for an hour with Diane, there was also a confidence that she did know what she was doing and, actually, we would never have to call the ambulance (if for no other reason than it wouldn't do her reputation any good).

God can be trusted; I worship the creator of the universe, a universe which our scientists still can't fully explain. I worship a God who created humankind. The human body is a phenomenal piece of engineering which, second after second, pumps blood, inhales and expels air, manages stress, creates desire and can be pushed to extremes. If you don't believe how finely balanced we are, stop breathing for a minute and see how it all goes wrong. The Bible tells me that I need not worry about tomorrow, for if God can care for the lilies of the fields, how much more will he care for me, when I am so much more important!?[57]

But stuff happens, and it can be easy to get anxious. Here is an extract from a report I was reading just as I wrote these words. The names and locations have been changed (to protect me!).

Week 13

Mr Code, a land officer in-charge of Central Bombay on Wednesday 8 May was introduced to us by our lawyer. (We are not working with the Peru one, since she is corrupt.) Gave him all copies of our documents. Said: when he

---

57 Matthew 6: 25–34.

finalizes, an officer called Jane Austin, the Chief Lands registrar, would sign the extension on or before 8 May.

Week 14

Jane Austin was arrested by Ethics and Anti-corruption police unit for signing title deeds, against the constitution.

As I read week 13, I felt encouraged that we were getting somewhere, then I read week 14 and felt we must have gone back to week 1, or even week -1.

Most people looking at Hand in Hand might imagine that we are a raging financial success. It is a complete waste of time telling people that we have no money, because nobody believes me. Of course, in one sense people are right not to believe me: for some, having no money means they don't eat; the difference when I say that we have no money is that we have always had access to money.

When I was new in Kenya, I used to stay with friends on my regular trips. I would go to meetings and take handwritten notes, and then come back to my friend's house in the evening and transfer my notes to the laptop. The friend I was staying with said to me one evening,

Why do you do that?

Me: *I don't like getting my laptop out in meetings; it's like I am showing off my wealth.*

My friend: *You fly in and out of the country every month, you wear a watch and you have white skin, everybody knows you are wealthy, whether you get your laptop out or not. Get over yourself.*

And of course, in one sense, he is correct. But I can tell you that there have been times when we have come to the end of the month and there has been no money for salaries. Any of you in business know what that means. There have been deals which should have taken weeks, but have taken years. Even the transfer of funds, which should be a simple process taking a couple of hours, can sometimes seem to take forever.

We commenced a housing project in Kenya in 2008, we allowed 1 year for procurement and 2 years for implementation. 7 years later, we are still on site, and have not sold all the houses. In my simple economist mindset, supply and demand tells us, therefore, that the price is too high; but every selling agent tells me that this is not the case. I assume, then, that the product must be shoddy and nobody wants it, but every selling agent tells me the houses are quality, the environment is great, there is nothing wrong with the product.

Then tell me,

WHY AREN'T THEY SELLING?!

We don't know.

Obviously the longer this goes on, the more we pay in finance, the less viable the project is, the less money HiH make to put into other projects and good causes. If paying more for finance means HiH make less and Grant Smith earns less and has one less holiday a year or has to sell the Land Cruiser (which he doesn't have) or has to live in a smaller house, I can do that. But this process ultimately rocks all that HiH want to achieve; and I know that it is business, and I know business is tough, and I know that just because I am a Christian does not mean that everything will work out fine, and I know God can be trusted. But it just seems at times that it is like running up a mountain with a rucksack on your back with somebody putting an extra brick in the rucksack after every mile, and then the shoulder strap snaps, and you get a stone in your shoe, and your sunglasses steam up, and you stumble on a rock, and there is a leak in your water bottle, and your phone battery is flat and you have forgotten your mobile charger, and you have a headache and you dropped the paracetamol 2 days back and ...

Then I remember the words of one of our investors:

Grant, you have been round the Kenyan block, you haven't lost money (yet), you still have your enthusiasm, most people would have gone home by now.

And I think, *yep* – but the only reason I haven't gone home is that I lost the ticket up the bloody mountain.

And then someone invariably asks me about what I do and what success looks like, and I might say it looks like Mary. Mary was a young lady with a difficult background and a desire to become an accountant. Mary studied accountancy at a project supported by Hand in Hand Charity. Having completed her qualifications, Mary was able to get a job in accountancy and subsequently sponsored herself and her sister into further education. Mary is now a senior accountant with HiHG in Nairobi.

Or I might say it looks like Raymond. He was going through university in Nairobi, studying construction and engineering, and came to us to work as an apprentice in CMS Africa. After he graduated, we had an opening for an additional Clerk of Works and so employed Raymond as an assistant, training him under our senior Clerk of Works. We are now furthering his training to facilitate Raymond to become whatever he chooses within the construction industry. If he wants my job, let him go for it; I won't stand in his way.

~~~~~~~~~~~~~~~~~~~~~~~~~~~~

At this point I have to stop and remember what God has done:

- HiH charity supporters trust us with £300k–£400k every year.
- The charity makes a difference to 3,000 children every year, year on year.
- HiH business have completed 120 high-end houses, and sold most of them.
- We are partnering a construction company that is implementing strong business ethics in their employment criteria.
- We have several significant investors who are willing to invest in our vision.
- Currently we are finalizing investments for £20m and £5m, which will create 600 jobs, 60 apprentices, and strengthen 4 Christian ministries as an outcome.
- We have numerous projects, like the above, and have potential investors prepared to commit to some of these projects.
- We are discussing with investors the reality of providing housing for Kenyans who live on less than £1.50 per day.

- HiH have made a few wise land purchases which have grown in value.
- Sue still loves me!

Therefore, as I look at the above, what do I conclude? We worship a God who is capable of anything we throw our imagination at. So, when we doubt or get frustrated, are we questioning the integrity of God?

As a young boy I memorized Micah 6:8

And what does the LORD require of you?
To act justly and to love mercy
and to walk humbly with your God.

What does it mean to act justly and to love mercy? I believe it is using our talents, our skills and our abilities to contribute to bringing God's kingdom here on earth. 'And to walk humbly with your God', well that is a bit easier: just do as we are told by the Almighty and surrender our lives to be who God wants us to be.

In John 5:36, Jesus tells us:

'*… For the works that the Father has given me to finish –*
the very works that I am doing – testify that the Father has
sent me.'

What we do is testimony to our Father; what is your testimony?

Last Sunday we sang in Church,

When Satan tempts us to despair,[58]

I believe that is an accurate description of a common experience.

The classic example is Elijah. One day he is standing on the top of a mountain with thousands of doubters who that day are going to find out that God is God.[59] Elijah knows it; he is at the peak of his trust in God. Elijah lays down a challenge to the prophets of the false gods,

Erect an altar and pray to your gods to ignite it with fire.[60]

Elijah is confident this won't happen, and he taunts the prophets of the false gods: *shout louder, shout longer.* You can imagine him pacing up and down, laughing and being sarcastic, because he is so sure of himself. But that is the easy bit, because after the prophets of the false gods lie exhausted and dejected with failure, it is Elijah's turn.

Elijah is 100% confident God is going to ignite the altar. So confident that he drenches the altar in water, asks God to come and the altar is engulfed in an inferno. Can you imagine how stupid Elijah would have looked, having goaded and taunted the prophets of the false gods all day and then drenching the altar in water, if fire had not come?

He would have been slaughtered, ripped limb from limb because he had made so many people look stupid. In fact, I am sure it was only God that protected him from not being slaughtered even when he was right. Not only that, which

---

58 From the hymn, *Before the Throne of God Above*, by C. L. Bancroft.

59 1 Kings 18.

60 1 Kings 18:25, my paraphrase.

was massive on its own, but then comes the rain which Elijah had stopped, or rather God had stopped, and the heavens open just as Elijah had said. It hadn't rained for 3 years; this is not a coincidence!

Here is Elijah, brimming with confidence in the Lord – he could have taken on giants, fought lions, raised the dead. He was God's chosen. And the next day he is running for his life from the queen, Jezebel, because he knows she wants him dead.

The day before, he angered thousands.

The day before, he made prophets look like idiots and completely undermined their assumed authority.

The day before, he had been so arrogant for God.

The day before, his life was under threat from almost everyone up that mountain.

So how do we understand that day? The day when we are told that Elijah runs for his life because he is afraid of the Queen and hides in a cave? He hears the voice of doubt, that asks:

Really?

That is the power of darkness.

I said at the beginning that I wanted you, the reader, to be reminded that God can use anyone – that there is nothing special about me. Can you see, there is nothing special about me, or Elijah, or Mary, or David; we are just tapping into a fraction of what God can do, and so can you. I also said at the beginning that I felt that, for so many of us, our full potential is untapped. The reason I believe that to be the case is because we hear that voice which says,

Really?

I believe the reality is that, too often, Satan's questioning tempts us to despair. We are afraid of failure, afraid of looking stupid, afraid of running out of money, afraid of getting it wrong, afraid of misunderstanding God's voice, of doing the wrong thing, of even not having enough faith. I am not sure any of this has anything to do with your (or my) level of faith. I think it is us listening to that voice! And we hear it louder than God's. That's why we have to encourage each other all the time, because we have to combat the numerous times we hear,

Really?

I have said that one of the reasons HiHG are where we are is because of the support, belief and encouragement of Timothy, Nancy, Charles, Marg, Joy, Jonathan, Calisto, Richard, Mark, Gordon, Ben, Dan, Gladys, Andrew, Bryan, Chizah, Jon, Jon, Mark, David, Stuart, Scott, Barry, Barrie, David, Emma, Joshua, Mwangi, Clive, Neil, Emmah, James, Peter, Jeanette, Phil, Guy, Vanda, Neil, Dan, Jon, Peter, Lorilee, Mike, Dave, Andy, Barney, Charity …

There are so many stories about so many people who have supported me. Some of them are in this book, some of them have dropped out of the book through the editing process, but they are all important stories of how I was picked up when I was down, or I was carried when I was high. Listed above are some of the people that, in one way or another, have encouraged me onto the next step. So many people in my life have been so important and probably most of them have no idea just how much impact they have had. It is impossible to do justice to all of you in these few pages, and so I express a deep thanks now.

Who has God put in your life that you need to encourage, affirm and support – even those who stand at that top of the mountain shouting for God, brimming with confidence, who you think need no support? They are the ones you ring and say,

You're doing a great job, do more.

Because they are hearing,

Really?

And too often they – we – are listening!

The reality for you and me is, at the end of the day, we have to make a choice. I have come to the conclusion that all of us justify what we do, how we do it, what we give our time to, how we spend our money. It's not that we purposely turn our back on God, or live a life that we know is wrong. It's that we calculate the parameters that work for us and are comfortable in that space. My final challenge to you, as well as myself, as a person who calls Jesus 'Lord' is: how far did Jesus go for me? Because I don't understand how privileged my life is, but I do know I am privileged and I don't know why. But if being a disciple of Jesus means anything to me, and knowing that Jesus went 'all in' for me (and theologically I understand that Jesus would have done that even if I was the only one), then I realize that all the stories of my life still go nowhere near reaching what Jesus did for me. And the same applies to you, whether you are a person that respects Jesus in your life or not, the fact that you are able to read this book suggests you too are very privileged. And the question has to be: so in my privileged status, what can I do to make a difference in others' lives?

So we both have a choice, and fundamentally that choice is: how far do I want to go? I don't think we will be punished to stay where we are, I don't think we will become more privileged if we do more. I guess it comes down to our police inspector who said,

Mum always taught me to do the right thing.

You, me, what's the right thing?

You see often, and I stress *often*, my battle is not with the bank or the Land Office or the contractor; my battle is a spiritual battle. And as I reflect on this, I know God has left me his Holy Spirit to defeat evil. That is why my potential, and yours, is largely untapped: because we allow evil to win these spiritual battles; yet if we understood who some of these battles are with, we would realize we can't lose because the odds are so stacked in God's favour. It's like the local under 5s football team playing Man U.

If Christians lived in the authority of the Spirit of God, and understood that often we are in a spiritual battle and that evil can't win, the world would be a different place.

The conclusion that I come to is that if we abandon our lives to the authority of the Holy Spirit, we will never reach our full potential. Yes, you read that correctly, you and I will never reach our full potential.

Why?

Because if we are completely submissive to what God can do, God can always take us further than we can ever imagine, plan or dream. There is always more.

And then I realize the title to the chapter is wrong. God *can* be trusted. And it's not so much that he makes it hard, it's that *I* make it hard.

~~~~~~

SOME LAST POINTS TO PONDER

- With God anything can be done.
- God can use anyone.
- What is there to be afraid of?
- If you are going to challenge someone, don't do it at the top of a mountain.

FINAL NOTE FROM GRANT

I hope you have enjoyed reading my words, although enjoyment may not be the most appropriate description. If you have questions you would like to ask, or areas of clarification or points you want to ponder, please don't hesitate to contact me:

grant@handinhandgroup.com

APPENDIX

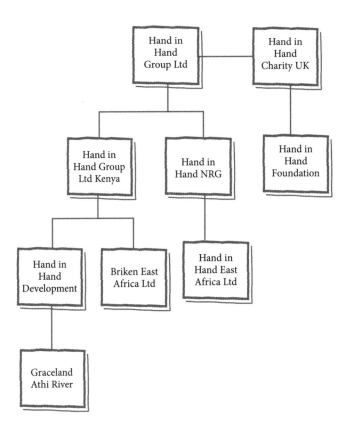

Hand in Hand Group Ltd (HiHG)

UK registered, umbrella company for all activity. Currently 3 directors, prior to 2017 managed by a voluntary management board.

Hand in Hand Group Ltd Kenya (HiHG Kenya)

Brand office of Hand in Hand Group Ltd UK.

Hand in Hand Development (HiHD)

Kenyan registered, 2 directors; 1 Kenyan, 1 UK. Undertakes housing projects.

Graceland Athi River (GAR)

Kenyan registered company. Joint Venture between Graceland Holdings and Hand in Hand Developments. Project company to build 230 houses.

Briken East Africa Ltd (Briken)

Kenyan registered company. 2 Directors; 1 Kenyan, 1 UK. Development manager for city projects.

Hand in Hand NRG (HiH NRG)

UK registered company, 2 UK directors. Purpose and investment company raising finance for Hand in Hand East Africa.

Hand in Hand East Africa Ltd (HiH EA)

Kenyan registered company, 2 directors; 1 Kenyan, 1 UK. Activity was growing jatropha oil.

Hand in Hand Charity UK (HiHC)

Registered with Charities Commission. 6 UK Trustees.
Role to raise awareness and resources for projects in Kenya
and Uganda.

Hand in Hand Foundation (HiHF)

Kenyan registered NGO (non-government organisation).
5 directors; 4 Kenyan, 1 UK. Is responsible for governance
and operations in Kenya and Uganda.

Muddy
Pearl